Lakeland Mountain Challenges

First published in 1999 by Grey Stone Books

British Library Cataloguing in Publication Data

A catalogue record of this book is available from the British Library.

ISBN 0-9515996-8-2

Printed by Carnmor Print and Design London Road, Preston

While every effort has been taken by the authors to ensure the accuracy of this book, changes do occur, and these may affect the contents. Neither the author nor the publisher accepts liability for these.

It is expected that walkers and climbers, or their companions, will be fully experienced in mountaincraft before setting out on the more serious expeditions.

Lakeland Mountain Challenges

A Guide for Walkers and Fellrunners

By Ronald Turnbull and Roy Clayton

Maps, sketches and line drawings by John Gillham

Grey Stone Books
Hoddlesden

Acknowledgments

We thank Bill Stainton and Vicki Farrar of the Ramblers' Association for information about the 3000s Marathon, and all the marshals and organisers of the 1997 event.
Thanks to the Ordnance Survey for an up-to-date copy of Outdoor Leisure 4, and to John Gillham of Grey Stone for impetus, maps, drawings, some photos and companionship on the hill.
Roy Clayton: I would like to thank my brother, James for his chauffeuring services and for his good company on the hills; Gail Simpson for her encouragement, and for typing – her eight fingers proved much faster than my two; and finally, my dad, who died during the production of this book.

Ronald Turnbull wrote: History of High-level Lakeland; Midwinter Attempt on the Threethousands; The Four and More; The Old County Tops; The Great Horseshoes Overview, including the Wasdale and Caldew circuits; Guidance.
Roy Clayton wrote: The Roy Story and the route description for the Lakes 3000s; Roamin' with the Romans; The Buttermere Horseshoe route; Penrith to the Sea

Photos:
Front Cover: Striding Edge in Winter by Jon Sparks Photography, Lancaster
Back cover: Mickledore and Scafell by Ronald Turnbull
Others: James Clayton: page 41; Roy Clayton 50, 80, 83, 112; John Cleare 17; John Gillham, 94, 102, 124, 132, 134, 136, 146; Nicola Gillham 10; Jon Sparks, 60; Ronald Turnbull 21, 24, 26, 31, 45, 53, 72, 128

The photos at chapter headings are of: Derwentwater and Grisedale Pike; Sunrise over Coniston Fells from Scafell; predawn on Skiddaw; Helvellyn Lower Man snowscene; Helvellyn shelter cairn; Kentmere from Mardale Ill Bell; Wastwater from Gable Climbers' Traverse; Roy's tent near High Park; Bowscale Fell to Blencathra. They were taken by Ronald Turnbull, Roy Clayton and John Gillham.

Contents

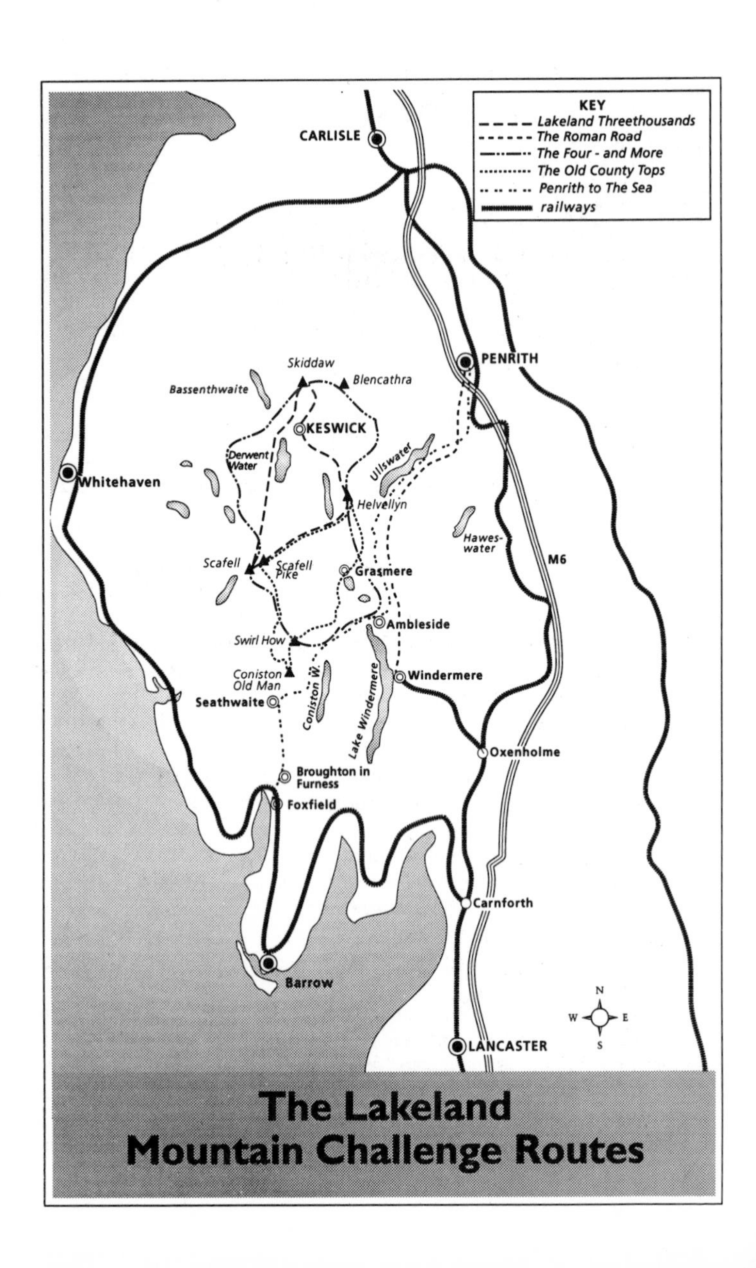
KEY
Lakeland Threethousands
The Roman Road
The Four - and More
The Old County Tops
Penrith to The Sea
railways
CARLISLE
PENRITH
Skiddaw
Blencathra
Bassenthwaite
KESWICK
Derwent Water
Ullswater
Whitehaven
Helvellyn
Hawes-water
M6
Scafell
Scafell Pike
Grasmere
Ambleside
Swirl How
Coniston Old Man
Windermere
Seathwaite
Coniston W.
Lake Windermere
Oxenholme
Broughton in Furness
Foxfield
Carnforth
Barrow
N
W
E
S
LANCASTER
The Lakeland Mountain Challenge Routes

INTRODUCTION

There are many reasons for walking on hills: the scenery, the companionship, the satisfaction of tricky compass work in mist. There is, dare I mention, the simple pleasure of showing off one's stylish and astonishingly waterproof Triplepoint Ceramic jacket. But nearly all of us, sooner or later, want to undertake a long and demanding walk just to see if we can do it.

Maybe it's the 45-mile Lyke Wake Walk, or the Yorkshire Three Peaks; maybe it's the Welsh Threethousands, or Tranter's Walk in Lochaber. However, for many of us the best walking in England (the best walking in the World?) is among the mountains of Lakeland.

The obvious long walk in Lakeland is the one over the four threethousands. Each of the four is a fine mountain, and they are fine in different ways. Skiddaw is grassy and isolated, its long slopes dropping to the Keswick Plain. Helvellyn is crag-sided, but with wide easy paths across its meadow-like summit. Scafell is crag-sided but also crag-topped, and all of its various approaches are difficult and spectacular. Scafell Pike is possibly the least interesting of the four, but it is the highest in England.

The threethousands are well spread out; if we did manage to do them all, we'd walk across four different volumes of Wainwright and look down into most of the Lakeland valleys. Our friends have been up the four on separate expeditions, and when we've succeeded they'll be able to say "Coo, gosh!" from a standpoint of knowledge and experience.

So it's not surprising that the circuit of the four attracts several hundred each year in the event organised by the Ramblers' Association, as well as uncounted freelances over the rest of the year. The walk has, however, a couple of drawbacks. The route is not ideal. It involves an inelegant out-and-back on Skiddaw's Tourist Path, and a long roadwalk up Borrowdale, as well as a shorter but nastier one along the A591. Secondly, the route is rather long: between forty and forty-five miles, depending on who's doing the measuring. On the first count, we have offered alternatives so that virtually the whole of the route can be accomplished off-road. The walk by woodland and lakeside, along the other side of Borrowdale, adds nothing to the length, and with its help the route becomes a mix of crag and valley, sheltered and fierce. Further improvement could only be achieved by moving Helvellyn five miles closer to Keswick, and that is beyond the powers of the present authors.

So we looked for a very long, very good walk that is yet not quite so long as forty-five miles. It wasn't hard to find it. The walk of Scafell Pike, Helvellyn and Coniston Old Man may lack the compelling logic of the four threethousands, but is not altogether arbitrary as these are the summits of the three former counties of Cumberland, Westmorland and Lancashire. The 35-mile tour of these three is, to my mind, even better than the longer one of the four. Borrowdale is good, but it isn't as good as Upper Eskdale. Derwentwater is a fine lake, but I'd trade it for the tarns of Grisedale, Seathwaite, and Little Langdale, and then we get our lake anyway at Grasmere.

A walk can be a lot shorter than these two and still be a long one. We can only guess what the Romans thought of the high traverse from Windermere to Penrith, but for walkers of today it has a railway station at each end, six peaks in the middle and a narrow grassy edge joining the whole thing together. It makes a fine outing if you're building fitness for the Threethousands or the Old County Tops, and is equally fine if you aren't...

At around the twenty-mile mark, the classic outing must be the circuit of one of the main valleys. We round them up into one convenient chapter. With them thus gathered into a tight space, we can lean over the railings like Cumbrian farmers at Penrith Mart and assess their undoubted merits; and pick out three of the best, the trips round Buttermere, Wasdale and Caldew.

At barely twenty miles, these last long routes run the risk of appearing almost short. So, finally, we expand and go multi-day. Those who walk the hills still only half-know them if they don't also sleep among them at night. On the trip from Penrith to the sea that sleeping is in bunkhouses and B&Bs, or in Lakeland's ancient inns. The trip of the Four and More is designed for a different and increasingly popular form of accommodation. The room decor is more impressive than at the Lodore Stakis; the beds less comfortable than the most primitive bunkhouse; and the cold shower before breakfast is something you get whether you want it or not – when you take your green breathable bag onto the summit of Gable or Haystacks, Grey Knotts or Sheffield Pike.

Ronald Turnbull, Thornhill 1998

The Moot Hall at Keswick may not the most spectacular building in the world, but if you have climbed England's four highest peaks and walked the best part of fifty miles to get to it, then it looks pretty damn good. It was a few minutes after midnight. I was tired, bordering on delirious. My throat was so dry that I could hardly speak, and all my muscles ached – even the ones I hadn't used. Tradition dictates that you run the last bit to the Moot Hall, but all I could muster was a drunken stagger. It had taken almost twenty-one and a half hours, but at last I had purged myself of the walk of the Lakeland Threethousands.

My idea of a day on the fells had changed a bit in the twenty years since I first ventured onto the Cumbrian mountains, on a school trip to the Langdale valley. I was enthusiastic and eager to impress, so when offered a choice of walks graded from easy to strenuous I chose the most challenging. Even without the other three threethousands, Scafell Pike was certainly a vigorous beginning for an inexperienced schoolboy. Not only did the rigours of Rossett Gill forever etch themselves in my memory, but the scorching July sun left me with a severely sunburned legs.

Sore and red though they may have been, I determined that those legs should carry me up every mountain in the Lake District. I began reading all the books I could find on the area. New libraries were built with the fines I incurred for late returns. I read about a man called Joss Naylor who had run 63 Lakeland fells, covering 92 miles in under 24 hours. He had dismissed the Pennine Way in a little over three days by giving up luxuries – such as sleep.

I became intrigued by these fell runners. They always seemed inappropriately dressed in trainers, T-shirts and the skimpiest of shorts, regardless of weather. While I struggled up hills puffing and wheezing like an asthmatic donkey, they would breeze past effortlessly with a cheery "morning". They could run, breathe, eat and – most irritating of all – smile, at the same time.

My fitness improved with each walk, although I soon realised that I was never going to be a Naylor. What is a doddle for one walker will

Roy Clayton (left) and Ronald Turnbull

be a challenge for another. In this book, our attitude is that when you set out, not just for an enjoyable day, but to see just how far and fast you can go, then that's a challenge walk. For an ordinary, not particularly fit, walker, that challenge could be the twenty-five mile Roman Road from Windermere to Penrith, or one of the great valley horseshoes. For a strong walker at the end of a fortnight of long hill days, it might be the Old County Tops, or the circuit of the four threethousands: Skiddaw, the Scafells and Helvellyn. For a fellrunner it will be the forty-two tops of the Bob Graham Round. And for Joss Naylor, all of these are pleasant easy days out in the hills.

The established walk of the Lakeland Threethousands is not as popular as its Welsh equivalent, covered in our previous book, *The Welsh Three Thousand Foot Challenges*. With the exception of the Scafells, the Lakeland version lacks the brutal rocky landscapes and cutting edge of the Welsh Threes. It is almost twenty miles longer – though this could be seen as an advantage, as the initial climb of Skiddaw in the dark adds greatly to the atmosphere of the undertaking. Most of all it incorporates two long sections of road walking. However, our route replaces the road sections with forest paths and lakeside trails, and manages to do this without increasing the overall length by more than half a mile.

Every year, some two hundred walkers and runners take part in the Ramblers' Association package tour around the four threethousands. Their valuable back-up, plus the presence of so many fellow-sufferers, provides very useful encouragement. We have included information on this event.

For the average walker, the shorter long walks could be used to build up strength and confidence for the really long ones. Longer walks not only require physical fitness and stamina, but mental preparation – and even a little science. Just how much pain and discomfort are you prepared to tolerate in order to reap the rewards? Certainly the appalling weather of 1998 tested my own resolve.

The science is provided in the form of Ronald's advice on diet and preparation. Ronald is an experienced runner with an appetite for distance events, and I have found his tips useful in pushing myself those extra miles. We hope that you enjoy reading about, and undertaking, the challenges as much as we have enjoyed setting them out for you.

Roy Clayton, Fleetwood 1998.

How to use the book

All distances have been measured directly off the 1:25,000 maps and no extra has been added for wiggles, effort, slope etc. So our miles are longer than some people's, though at least they should all be roughly the same as each other. On the Threethousands walk, however, we have added 5% to distances so as to reach the 'traditional' length of 45 miles.

The sketch-maps and drawings should always be supplemented with a properly surveyed map. For straightforward ridge-walks the 1:50,000 Landranger is adequate; for trickier work off the main paths we recommend either the Harveys maps or the 1:25,000 Outdoor Leisure series. On all high-level routes walkers should have basic fellcraft, such as the use of the compass in mist, and sufficient judgment to turn back should the weather and the condition of the party require it.

A long-distance challenge under Winter conditions is specially rewarding, but requires special skills. Swirral Edge, for instance, can become a proper ice-climb. Please read carefully the notes in the 'Guidance' chapter before considering such an attempt. Our route descriptions assume the fells snow-free and unfrozen.

A History of High-Level Lakeland

It takes a leap of faith to believe that a human being can walk forty miles or more over hills, and even enjoy doing so. That leap of faith – that stride into the unknown – came early in Lakeland. In 1870, when a high circuit of Wasdale by the Scafells, Gable and Pillar was considered just about the most the human boot could tread over in a day, Mr Thomas Watson and the guide Thomas Wilson of Borrowdale walked a circuit similar to the modern Threethousands. They didn't include Scafell, considering it a mere outlier of the Pikes; on the other hand they did include Blencathra (which in those days was called Saddleback by everyone except Wordsworth). So their route was longer and harder than ours, and they covered it in nailed boots, passing through thick mist during the night, snow showers on Scafell Pikes and gales that forced them to crawl to the cairn on Saddleback. But most of all, they overcame the long-standing belief that such a route could not be walked.

Some walkers may feel a bit pleased with themselves at having covered the Threethousands. This feat of 1870 is just the start of a sequence of historical humiliations in store for those walkers. The sturdy Victorians outdid each other in the number of hills covered.

Lawrence and Charles Pilkington, with Matt Barnes, the guide, walked an extended round including Great Gable in 24hrs 25min. The Pilkington brothers are more famous for their first ascent of the Inaccessible Pinnacle on Skye in 1880.

In the 1890s John Wilson Robinson used to walk from his home at Lorton for a day's climbing at Wasdale Head – twelve miles each way, with Great Gable obstructing the route. So it's hardly surprising that on a day in October 1893 when the conditions didn't favour rock climbing he had a go at the Threethousanders. It was snowy so he and

G B Gibbs carried alpenstocks, and needed them on the Scafells. Robinson lowered Gibbs down Broad Stand by his rucksack straps; as he dangled, Gibbs kicked the ice off the holds for Robinson to follow. This is the man commemorated at Robinson's Cairn, which is passed on the Wasdale Horseshoe walk. He was third on the rope (behind Collie) on one of Lakeland's nicest climbs – Moss Ghyll on Scafell – and also on one of the nastiest – Great Gully on the Screes.

In 1905 Dr A W Wakefield of Keswick crossed the Threethousands, with the addition of Dale Head, Great Gable, Pillar and Steeple, Red Pike and Yewbarrow; Bowfell; Fairfield and Blencathra; and various lesser heights. His time for the circuit was 22 hrs 7 minutes.

He was an interesting chap, this Dr Wakefield. He was a GP in Keswick, and swam in Derwentwater every day. For his long walk he wore shorts, rubber shoes and his old Sedbergh school rugger jersey. (Lightweight tennis shoes were now widely used on harder rock climbs.) He was also a rock climber, and took part in various classic first ascents, though always as second (his leader was G S Bower). In 1920 they climbed Ash Tree Slabs on Gimmer, a delightful route now graded Severe – what a privilege to be first up that. So impressive were these Lakeland achievements that he was invited onto the Everest expedition of 1922, even though he was then 45 years old. He reached Camp 3, 1000ft below the North Col, but suffered at altitude.

In the 1920s one could be at the forefront in all branches of mountaineering – Himalayan, rock-climbing and fellrunning – but this of course is only possible when few are active and standards are low.

During the next fifty-five years, this 'Lakeland 24-hour Record' was broken just twice. In 1920 Eustace Thomas of the Rucksack Club completed the Wakefield round in 21 hrs 25. He was over 50 at the time. In 1921 he added the ridge north from Helvellyn over the Dodds. (Thomas, a Manchester businessman, also held records in the Pennines and Scotland, and over the Welsh 3000s; and was the first Englishman to ascend all of the Alpine 4000m peaks.)

And then, in June 1932, Bob Graham, a guest-house keeper from Keswick, circled 42 hills, adding in the Langdale Pikes and Great Calva, a heathery thing at the Back of Skiddaw.

Bob Graham left the Moot Hall at 1:00 am on a fine June night. "The uphill bits gave me a rest, and if I felt tired going up I thought to myself: I can always get a rest running down the next bit." In other words, the entire trip consisted of rest! (Actually this is not as silly as it sounds.) The year before, when he was only 41, he'd failed to complete a 41-top circuit. This time, a year older, he needed an extra summit.

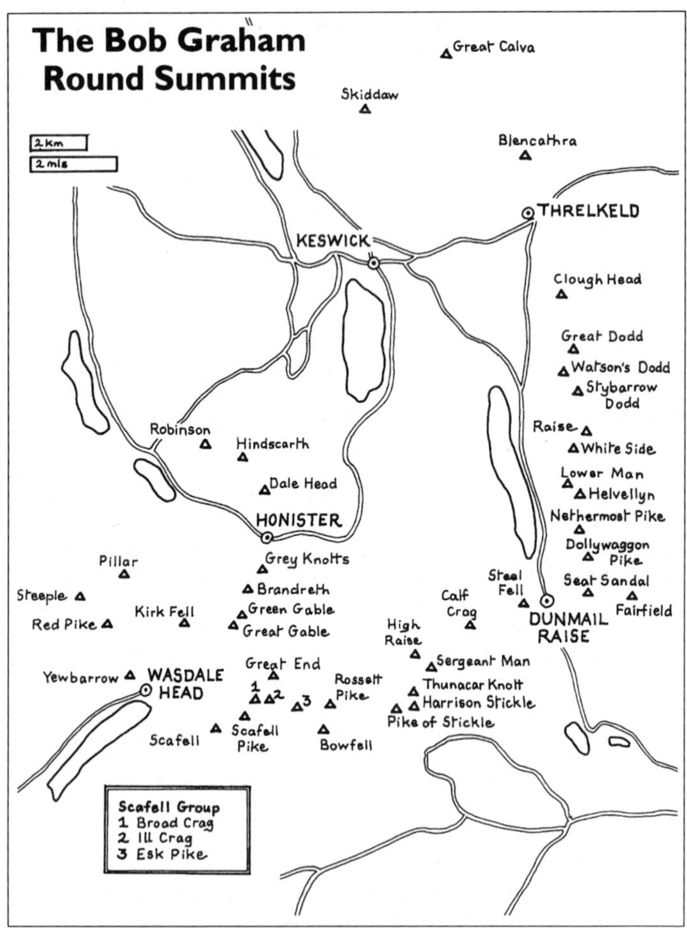

His sporting choice was Calva, with its 800 feet of extra climb.

He ran in shorts, pyjama jacket and gym shoes; he dined on bread and butter, lightly-boiled egg, and sweets. At Dunmail Raise he was photographed by the Abraham Brothers. The weather closed in: heavy rain on Red Pike, mist on the Derwent fells, also thunder and lightening. He reached Newlands Hause at midnight, and ran the last 7 miles down the road in 39 minutes. He lost half a stone on his run and was up at six next morning making breakfast for his support team.

"What were you thinking about?" Harry Griffin asked him once. "Oh, I'd no time to do much thinking. We were laughing and telling tales all the way. We thought it great fun. Yes, it was a good day."

The stout Victorians had overcome the prejudices of their time: prejudices that are, indeed still with us. 'Always wear boots'; 'it's vulgar to run'; as well as the more inclusive 'hills not some infernal racetrack' and 'just not possible'. In Wales at the same time, the knocking-down of the local Threethousands took place amid recriminations, controversy and fuss. Lakeland was more tolerant. Lakeland hadn't minded Wordsworth striding up and down Easedale reciting his own poetry in a loud voice. Lakeland has put up with people trying to reach the speed of sound in boats. In Lakeland, running up mountains was already an established sport for dogs and humans, and a country that competes in making horrible faces through a horse-collar isn't going to be bothered about a bit of hillwalking.

Bob Graham's trip was not all that much longer than Dr Wakefield's one: it's a mere mile further, although the total ascent has increased from 22,000ft (Kilimanjaro) to 27,000ft (Everest). Having broken through the Victorian belief barrier, Graham seemed to have reached the limit of human ability in this particular game. His record remained unequalled for nearly 30 years. The serious peakbagger of 1960 could safely reckon that 42 must be about it.

But that safe reckoning would have been quite wrong. As roadrunners want to run the Marathon, as hillwalkers want to walk the Welsh or the English Threethousands, as mountaineers want to achieve the Skye Ridge, so Bob Graham's circuit has become the standard test for the ordinary, middling fellrunner of today. Each year some hundred of us attempt this formerly ultimate circuit, and some fifty of the hundred achieve it.

Are we so much fitter than our forefathers? Or do we just have bigger feet? We are a bit fitter than our forefathers – we have more time to train. Our feet are bigger – we have better food. But mostly, we're better educated. We know about dehydration, we know how to train for endurance, we know how to pace ourselves along the way. But most of all, we know it can be done; so we go out and do it.

Currently the Lake District 24-hour record stands at 78 summits. Why then is it Bob Graham's Round that has become the classic, rather than, say, Eric Beard's Round (56 peaks) or Joss Naylor's Round (72 peaks)? It's not just that it's the exact right length to be always possible but never probable. The Bob Graham Round is, on top of that (and on top of 42 other things as well) a superb day out.

Apart from the five road miles into Keswick, it spends the entire day and night on hill ground of the most attractive sort. There's rough heather at the back of Skiddaw, smooth grassy ridge-running along the Dodds, and miles of bare rock and boulder over the Scafells. There's easy but exciting scrambling on Blencathra and Kirk Fell, while a seasoning of fear is sprinkled onto the big meal of exhaustion when you get to the short rock climb of Broad Stand.

Walk, clamber and jog out of the darkness into the dawn; scamper down Halls Fell at sunrise. Stand above Langdale, and weave up through the crags on the steep side of Bowfell. Pass through the midday heat and drop into the deep hollow of Wasdale. Cross Gable in the silent empty evening and, as light fades, make your way down the long last spur of Robinson to where kind friends are waiting with glucose beside the little church.

Or else not – if you should meet bad weather or injury, or get the starting speed wrong, or eat too little or too much, or go off route. There is a list of the 42 tops, with advice on attempting them, in the final 'Twice as Far' section of the book.

Meanwhile the real runners head ever onwards and upwards. Joss Naylor comes into sight, recognisable even from a distance by his crouching gait. He looks unhealthily thin, and his legs do not bulge with muscles: they have been referred to as the 'Joss sticks'. But he comes downhill as elegantly as a fox, and there's nothing unhealthy about the way he disappears up the opposite slope.

Joss Naylor is a ready-made legend. He's been a Wasdale shepherd all his life (well, he spent several years as a fitter for British Nuclear Fuels at Sellafield, but the legend is big enough to ignore that). His sport was Cumberland wrestling, until a back injury laid him low for six months. At this point he made the odd, but obviously correct, decision to switch to fellrunning.

The Mountain Trial came to Wasdale. Joss entered it, ran in his work-boots, and led the field for the first couple of hills before going down with cramp. Two years later, he stayed in front all the way, to finish first by half an hour. He didn't win, though – he'd missed one of the checkpoints, even though it was in his home valley. He learned to read maps, learned about training, and went through the Lake District fell-running records like a collie through a flock of hens. He found the 24-hour record at 60 peaks, and raised it to 61, then 65, then 72. A trip round the Lakes Threethousands in 8½ hours was just a training

Joss Naylor Photo: John Cleare/ Mountain Camera Picture Library

run for one of these attempts.

In his final circuit he added to Bob Graham's 42 another six tops in the Skiddaw group, and a big drop into Langdale for Pike of Blisco and the Crinkle Crags; and a further eleven peaks in the Grasmoor group. He had covered over 80 miles of ground, with 37,000 feet of ascent. That's seven miles vertically upwards, enough to climb right off Planet Earth into the bottom of the stratosphere.

He did not restrict himself, however, to runs of a single day. He ran the Pennine Way in just over three, and in 1986 visited every one of the 214 summits in Wainwright's guides in one week, one hour and fifteen minutes. In 1996 he celebrated his sixtieth birthday by crossing the sixty Lake District summits of over 2500 feet. As so often, he outran the schedule, the pacers and the press. Is Walna Scar to the Three Shires Stone a good day's walk? It's two hours twenty minutes for Joss Naylor. The trip of 100 miles with 40,000 feet of ascent, from Dow Crag to Rampsgill Head, took him 36 hours and 50 minutes. I was one of a hundred runners younger than himself that Joss outran in the Mountain Trial the following year.

Lakeland shepherds are still among our top fellrunners, but they are joined by engineers and systems analysts from the Midlands and even the South of England. These people train, scientifically, on the track, and Joss Naylor's records are gradually starting to fall. The 24-hour record now stands at 78 tops; the Bob Graham Round has been run in 13 hrs 53 minutes (Billy Bland) and by a 14-year old (Ben Squibb).

Meanwhile the walkers continue to enjoy, or at least to achieve, their round of the Threethousands. For over 30 years now this has been organised as an annual challenge walk by the Rambler's Association, with some safely cover, eleven checkpoints, and food at Seathwaite and Steel End. Details of this event are in the final 'Twice as Far' section. The writer Harry Griffin, whose article in the Lancashire Herald in 1960 was the match to the blue paper of Bob Graham activity, himself walked the Threethousands in his late seventies with an older companion. On another occasion he happened to be, on the day of the Ramblers' Challenge, above Wythburn Church on the broad and popular path up Britain's most frequented hill.

"Is this the right way for Helvellyn?" The man who asked this surprising question was unfit, close to exhaustion, and wearing unsuitable shoes. Harry said that it was, and asked him how he was enjoying himself.

"It's been the best day of my life."

Humbled, Harry swallowed the remarks he'd been preparing about the necessity of maps, compasses and sensible short distances, and walked quietly off down Helvellyn.

The Roy Story

How had Turnbull managed to talk me into this one? Mathematics alone should have deterred me from such madness. A sixteen-hour schedule and forty-five miles requires an average foot speed of three miles an hour, and Ronald himself has a reputation for wearing out walking partners like a schoolboy wears out shoes. Although I had walked Ben Nevis, Snowdon, and Scafell Pike in preparation for the walk, I remained untested over such a long distance. I had also some pain from a recurring knee injury.

But here I was in the glow of a warm summer evening, stopping off at Wythburn car park to conceal some supplies for the last leg of the journey. "Something that you might fancy, but wouldn't like to carry," were Ronald's instructions. For me that would be fish and chips and a six-pack, but Ronald thought that some tins of rice pudding and glucose drinks would be more appropriate. How would we be feeling when we recovered them late the next afternoon?

Six hours later, after a brief sleep, the three of us stood beside the Moot Hall primed and ready to go. It was a clear starlit night with a refreshing breeze – perfect conditions for our attempt. "It is 2.20 am" snapped Ronald with alarming precision. He slapped the wall and set off like a bull terrier straining at the leash. We sped after him through the streets of Keswick, torches firmly clasped in hand. "It seems strange to be setting off at walking pace," Ronald laughed. Walking pace! I wouldn't move this fast if I were being chased by a pack of hungry wolves. I would have said so, but I was too busy drawing breath. Boyen appeared to have little problem with the pace and I suddenly felt quite intimidated.

Soon we were clear of the amber street-lights and ascending the tree-lined slopes of Latrigg. "Does anybody think we need the torches?" Ronald asked along one dimly lit stretch. Suddenly he fixed his beam on a gate that we were on collision course for. As he turned around and flicked the torch off again, I wondered if his facial expression was one of astonishment, or perhaps a wry knowing grin?

I was aware that Skiddaw was a shapely mountain with good views, but a tedious climb. In the darkness, though, there was something magical about it. Dancing black shadows of pine trees, the smell of damp ferns and the gurgling of streams accompanied the pounding of Vibram on stone. I was quite enjoying this.

The clues to our gaining height were the diminishing lights of Keswick and increasingly fresh winds. The open fells and the surrounding hills were various shades of grey, as was the barely discernible shoreline of Derwentwater.

At 4.30am we reached the top of Skiddaw, slightly ahead of our schedule and just in time to witness the pink ribbons of the sunrise over the Scottish Lowlands. The sun appeared to rise from several points, casting light and colour over the dull Derwent plains. Boyen was clearly not happy at having to expend so much energy on Skiddaw. A mountain of only nine hundred metres should have been much easier: Skiddaw wouldn't even rank as a hill in his native Slovenia.

It was starting to get light as we neared the foot of Carl Side and the village of Applethwaite. I felt a sense of satisfaction at sneaking up and down Skiddaw unnoticed, the only exception being a vigilant sheep-dog at Millbeck. Ronald disappeared into some fields to check out another path. We soon saw him sprinting through a pasture down below us. Boyen seemed relieved that he could slow the pace; "Ronald, he is very fast, very fit," he said in broken English, and then inquired about the direction of the car.

Portinscale was asleep: the cartons of milk still lined the doorsteps. Ronald had suggested that we spice the walk up a little by using tracks on the west bank of Derwentwater – Ronald doesn't like anything too easy. The forest paths were delightful: the sunlight pierced the trees and shimmered on the surface of Derwentwater. We stopped on the

Roy refuelling in Borrowdale

jetty for food and photos. Boyen's reluctance to repack his rucksack indicated that he was weakening. Had he underestimated the Lakeland Threes?

At eight we reached the camp-site in Borrowdale where we had spent the previous night (all three hours of it!) We rested beside our tents and filled our bellies before resuming our journey.

Seathwaite may be the wettest place in England, but today it was hotting up nicely for the Scafells. We were back into the serious stuff. Now we were joined by all the other walkers just beginning their day. As we headed uphill towards Taylor Gill Force we were surprised to meet walkers in descent, so early in the day. They stopped to warn us of strong winds on the higher ground. "Ya'll be needin' a big jacket," the large Geordie informed Ronald. Ronald resisted the temptation to tell him that we had already climbed one three-thousand footer and covered fifteen miles before breakfast, but found it hard to conceal his amusement that his attempt on the Lakeland Threethousands might be thwarted by the smallness of his jacket.

Unfortunately for Boyen the ascent of Sty Head proved to be the last straw. We were still less than half way, but a muscle strain forced

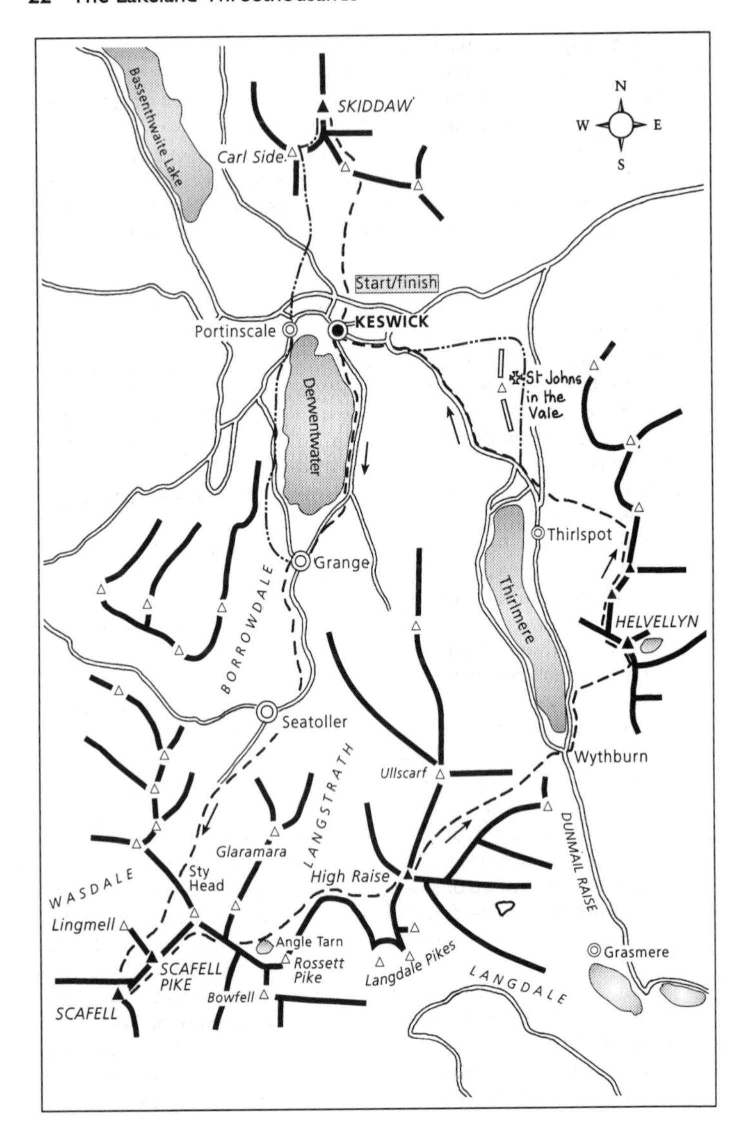
N
W
E
S
Bassenthwaite Lake
SKIDDAW
Carl Side
Start/finish
KESWICK
Portinscale
Derwentwater
St Johns in the Vale
Thirlspot
Thirlmere
Grange
BORROWDALE
HELVELLYN
Seatoller
LANGSTRATH
Ullscarf
Wythburn
DUNMAIL RAISE
Glaramara
Sty Head
High Raise
WASDALE
Lingmell
Angle Tarn
Rossett Pike
Langdale Pikes
SCAFELL PIKE
Bowfell
SCAFELL
LANGDALE
Grasmere

his retreat. Boyen dejectedly began his slow walk back to the campsite while we continued up the Sty Head pass.

Despite the ferocious pace, we had fallen behind our schedule by more than an hour, but the sight of Boyen retiring boosted my own confidence. I no longer felt so weak in comparison to these toughies and began to run along the pass with renewed vigour. Ronald was impressed and suggested that if I felt so fit I could carry the rucksack. This idea did not appeal and I decided that it would be wise to exercise some restraint.

We pressed on, dipping our heads and eager mouths into every stream of water and devouring home-made jam sandwiches without even stopping – serious fell runners don't, apparently!

The Corridor Route was frustrating. Scafell Pike was right beside us, but we had to by-pass it in favour of Scafell. Soon we reached Hollow Stones and gazed across at the mauve cliffs of Scafell Crag, our eyes tracing the impending route up Lords Rake. Many people argue that Scafell is a better mountain than the Pike and as I stood humbled beneath this bastion of rock, I had to agree – fellwalking doesn't get much finer than this.

Unfortunately we had to surrender some of the height gained so far, to reach the screes at the top of Brown Tongue. My strength began to desert me and my legs were shaking as we clambered up Lords Rake. Although I had eaten enough Muesli bars to qualify for a Swiss passport, I should have evidently eaten more. My uncle, John Gillham, has often commented on my miles to the Mars bar ratio. "If you were a car," he stated, "I would scrap you." Today I was having an uneconomical day. Also my right knee was starting to ache; however, we had a climb ahead that was even stiffer than my legs...

It had been a long time since our last summit and I was in need of a confidence boost. Soon my prayers were answered and I staggered onto Scafell within sight of the cairn. Ronald gave me a Mars bar, which I gratefully devoured and washed down with half a gallon of water and a couple of strong painkillers. My knee was hurting quite badly and I began to have doubts about finishing the walk. I feigned a smile for the summit photograph, and we began descending to Foxes Tarn.

At 2pm, almost twelve hours into the walk, we arrived at the monstrous cairn on Scafell Pike. We had little desire to stay on the overcrowded summit, even if we could have found space. "Three down one to go," I said to Ronald. Rather unconvinced, he smiled. Did I want to abandon the walk and head back to Borrowdale? I remembered some weeks earlier Ronald had sprained his ankle running on Coniston Old Man, but still finished off the entire range before returning home. I wished I had a reasonable excuse for giving up, like a broken leg. I didn't, so I declined the offer.

Roy on the Corridor Route

Before long the rocky debris of the Scafells gave way to the soft grasses of the central hills. The walk to Angle Tarn is pleasant and quite easy, but even the smallest undulation seemed taxing and the painkillers were not killing any pain.

Ronald had warned me not to underestimate High Raise. Its thousand-foot slope of depressing grass could prove more of an obstacle even than Helvellyn itself. The long spongy grass drained all my energy once again. Why not a Low Raise, I wondered.

We plodded on relentlessly but the summit appeared to get no nearer. Once again Ronald suggested returning along Langstrath and terminating the walk. I could not be beaten by the smallest hill of the day, a mere 2500-footer, so once again refused this tempting offer. Eventually we reached the elusive cairn and I could see the eastern fells and the taunting mass of Helvellyn in the middle. Now all I had to do was roll down to Thirlmere.

Many a summer walk has ended with a long march along a valley, but I cannot recall any as long and agonising as Wythburn on that day. My knee had locked, my foot was badly bruised, I had a stubbed toe and my soles were covered in blisters. My feet were rebelling and had assumed a life (or perhaps a death) of their own. The only acceptable route was the most direct one. Consequently I spent much of the time trying to extricate myself from knee-deep peat bogs. At least the brown-stained waters soothed my burning feet, but I finally accepted that the walk was over. Helvellyn, the easiest of the four, would beat me.

Ronald had already decided that if he reached Wythburn before 7pm he would continue up Helvellyn alone. At Wythburn Church we recovered our supplies and ate them in silence before Ronald and I parted company. As I waited at the roadside for a lift I imagined him striking clear of the pine forest onto the breast of Helvellyn and contemplated the lone descent he would have to make in the dark.

I did not have long to wait before a kindly farmer took pity at my dishevelled body slumped against the wall, thumb half cocked. "The dog doesn't like sharing the front seat," he explained, so I jumped into the open back of the Landrover. It was a rather undignified ending to the day I thought, being perched among buckets and toilet brushes in the back of a Landrover, but at least I could gaze upon Helvellyn as the sun began to set.

Days later the blisters had gone, weeks later the foot had healed, and after a couple of months of physiotherapy the leg was almost back to normal. Wounded pride takes longer to stop hurting. Almost a year passed before I started to be troubled by thoughts of a further attempt at the Lakes Threethousands.

Ronald had suggested that good company and free sandwiches might aid my chances. There may well be no such thing as a free lunch; but the 33rd Threethousands Marathon of the Ramblers' Association, during the wettest June ever, seemed a hell of a way to earn a few butties.

Two hundred walkers trotting through Keswick reminded me of the Spanish bull-running festival. Fitz Park in the dark – again! I wondered what it looked like in daylight, as we funnelled across the Greta footbridge into the blackness. The procession of torches up Jenkin Hill was spectacular, although the weather wasn't. By the time it started to get light I was soaked to the skin. Dark shadows hurtled out of the mist as the path finally flattened; the front runners were already coming down.

We had to reach Seathwaite before 9:30 or be timed out, so the march along Borrowdale was brisk. The rain stopped, the birds chattered and our optimism was renewed. A barn had been converted

Roy and Boyen at Stockley Bridge

into a welcome third checkpoint. The first walkers had passed through three hours earlier, just after 5:00, and there were only a few sandwiches left. Clouds of steam rose from the bare wrinkled feet of walkers checking for blisters.

I struggled up the water-logged paths to Sty Head like a spawning salmon heading upstream. Perhaps I could be the first to swim the Lakeland Threethousands...

The fast trek along the Borrowdale road had taken its toll. It was a slow drag to the foot of Scafell Crag. My legs quivered as they remembered the previous attempt. They – the legs – wanted to wait and compose themselves, but the head said there wasn't time. I practised moonwalking, Jackson-style, on the slippery screes, and followed Lord's Rake all the way.

After wandering through mists for several minutes I found the summit and set off for Scafell Pike. The gully from Foxes Tarn had filled with water and it poured into boots and socks. It took an age to get up the slippery rocks and find the cairn on the Pike. My schedule was in tatters. I had half an hour to get to Esk Hause or be withdrawn.

Each time I walk this section there are more ups and downs. I staggered drunkenly over the loose echoing boulders, and reached Esk

Hause, an hour too late, at 3:00pm. It was a long, long way down to Seatoller.

As I drove home along the Grasmere road I passed familiar faces: the man in the red fleece, some of the Geordies. They looked exhausted; but I would gladly have changed places as they marched triumphant towards Keswick, bathed in glorious evening sun.

Two months later I was back on Esk Hause. This time I'd avoided the previous mistakes – not eating enough, too fast along Borrowdale. At the same time I'd made one or two new ones – the ready mixed carbohydrate drink on Skiddaw that tasted a bit like washing up water – because it was washing up water! Two identical water bottles on the draining board, and the one with my complex carbohydrates wasn't going to get the dishes particularly clean.

I'd kept more-or-less on schedule all the way. At Stake Pass though, the afternoon sun was at its hottest, the breeze had vanished and there was a deathly silence, with the exception of a few twittering skylarks. Worse than washing-up water was no water at all: I'd allowed myself to run out, and the slow-flowing algae-infested waters above Langstrath looked distinctly unpalatable.

Ronald once said that this walk puts the hell in Helvellyn; it also puts the why? in Wythburn. The top and sides are nice, but the bottom is full of the worst slime known to man. Nothing was more certain than some of the evil stuff would find a way into my socks.

The valley was sheltered, but still hot. And the water was still a mucky brown. If I did not find water soon, I would be burnt out before Helvellyn. I managed to contact James on the CB and he told me that my cold cans of Lucozade were waiting. I begged him to bring them up to me, but he said no – or words to that effect! In the bottom of the valley I disturbed a courting couple behind a huge boulder. "Oh, I thought we were the last on the fells," the man explained sheepishly.

My brother James – and, more importantly, the Lucozade – were in the Wythburn car park. I had until now split the walk into imaginary manageable chunks and not let myself look at the big picture. My body still felt strong, but dehydration had weakened my spirit. Time was pressing and I had to make a quick decision, carry on or split. Ahead there was still 2500ft of torture. To climb Helvellyn and reach Keswick could be considered courageous, but to have to call out the mountain rescue would be foolish. Sense prevailed, and I decided to retire.

On the other hand I was at the bottom of Helvellyn, not seriously injured, and it wasn't dark yet. I was even carrying a radio – why, the

Mountain Rescue, when they came to get me, would think I'd been positively sensible!

I changed into dry socks and boots, then massaged my legs with deep heat cream. I drank two cans of Lucozade, ate some of my compressed lemon-cheese sandwiches and set off into the pine forests.

As I reached the open fell I met a party of walkers descending. "It'll be getting dark soon, are you going far?" one of the women inquired. "No, not far," I replied discreetly. "Oh, just out for a little bit of a stroll then. How nice." I decided to stuff modesty: "Yes, I've done Skiddaw, Scafell, and Scafell Pike, so I thought I'd finish with Helvellyn."

After they'd gone down off the mountain I began to feel rather lonely. The trees around Thirlmere blackened and the last rays of light faded as the sun slipped behind Grasmoor. Once up on the ridge I took a few last photos before exchanging the camera for the torch, and radio-ed James to tell him that Helvellyn was now in the bag.

What a silly thing to say. The normally easy paths along the top had been stretched to fit the occasion. Still, my watch told me that I was making good time. If so, it was more down to fear than to fitness.

Not surprisingly, there was no one else on the top. I had never before been alone on a summit in the dark: it was quite eerie. The powerful beam of James' torch made no impression on the blackness over the eastern edge.

It normally takes less than an hour to get down to Thirlspot, but this was not a normal time. I stopped every few yards to let my jelly legs stop shaking. It was almost 10pm by the time I reached the car park at Swirls. James removed one source of temptation by driving the car away to Keswick. The other temptation was the Kings Head, but that was a good twenty yards off route and I did not have the energy for any diversions.

I was a long time dreaming of those orange lights of Keswick, and I wished I had some company to share the moment of glory. It would have been nice to get round first time; but on the attempt with Ronald I had been simply not fit enough. It would have been wonderful to share the adventure and comradeship with a hundred Ramblers through the gales and lashing rain. These previous failures (or 'partial successes', as Ronald refers to them) served to sweeten my present achievement.

As I splodged onto the steps of the Moot Hall, just one question remained. Do I tell Turnbull what I've done – and risk him dreaming me up something even more dreadful than the Lakeland Threethousands?

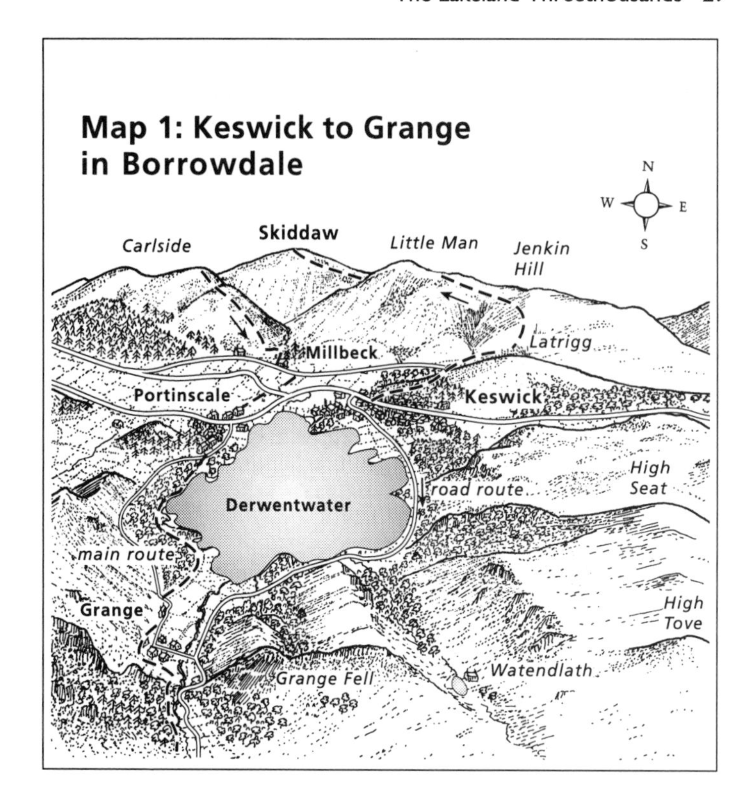

The Lakeland Threethousands – The Route

Distance 45 miles (72km): height gain 11,000 ft (3300m)

There are four mountains in England over three thousand feet high; Scafell Pike (3210ft), Scafell (3162ft), Helvellyn (3118ft) and Skiddaw (3054ft). There are other tops in excess of this height – Broad Crag (3054ft), Ill Crag (3040ft) and Helvellyn Low Man (3033ft) – but they do not qualify as separate peaks because of the insufficient drop in height.

For all but the fastest of runners at least one of the peaks will have to be scaled at night-time. Skiddaw, being the easiest and least treacherous of the four, is the usual choice. Tired feet are thus afforded the relatively safe descent of Helvellyn.

Our main route has all but eliminated road walking, replacing the 15km of Borrowdale and the 10km finale from Thirlspot with field paths, forest tracks and pleasant lakeside trails. The road routes are no shorter than our path alternatives, but they are slightly quicker: they are summarised at the end of the chapter. Within the text, various brief alternatives are in smaller type.

1: Skiddaw

Keswick to Portinscale (9 miles, 15km)

Skiddaw is the oldest mountain in the Lake District and was once thought to be higher than the Scafells. The name ('Skytja Haughr') is of Nordic origin, meaning Shooters' or Archers' Hill. The mountain was a popular guided excursion in Victorian times and the main path from Keswick is still referred to as the Pony Track. Although the route is generally well worn, it is tricky to find at the outset in the absence of signposts, and even more so at night.

The route begins and ends at the **Moot Hall**, Keswick. Go through the alley at the Golden Lion public house to reach the car park at the rear. Cross the car park diagonally slanting left to the main road where there is a signpost 'to Otley Road Long Stay Car Park'. Head down Otley Road as far as the first bend (between No 19 and the garages), to find a tarmac lane on the left. Follow the lane, which turns right, and then bear right at a dividing fence. The path descends to a footbridge spanning the River Greta and crosses to enter Fitz Park.

At the far left corner of the park is a three way path junction marked by a post. Take the left path, which leads to a roadside kissing gate. Turn right for 75yds, passing some new houses, to Spooney Green Lane. The lane can be identified by a public footpath sign marked 'to Skiddaw'. The wide gravel track crosses over the A66 via a footbridge and begins a moderately steep ascent, skirting the pine clad slopes of Latrigg. Where the track forks, take the more prominent left path along the top edge of the woods. There is a useful water source just before the gate on the last left-hand bend as you leave the trees.

Nearly two miles from the town centre the track emerges at a car park on the Gale Road. Go right to the stile at the end of the car park, where a the public footpath signpost points the way left. A narrow path beside barbed wire gently climbs the slopes of Lonscale Fell,

On Skiddaw's stony summit ridge

passing a memorial stone to the shepherds of the Hawell family, lost at the turn of the century. From here the path drops to a grassy col. The dip is a prelude to the steepest section of Skiddaw.

A badly eroded path splayed wide across the bracken slopes of Jenkin Hill gains three hundred metres in less than a mile. Fortunately in the dark it is not possible to gauge the steepness or witness how untidy the route has become. The path to the left follows a fence and is steeper than the firmer path on the right, which follows a clough near the former site of a refreshment hut. At the 450m contour a gate and stile are passed and the path veers left.

The gradient eases over the next couple of miles as a second gate is passed at the 800m contour. The path now rakes below Skiddaw Little Man for a mile (1.5km), ascending another 300ft (90m vertical) to the last gate and stile. The final section is steep, over loose shale to the southern extremity of Skiddaw's ridge. The main summit is a half-mile northwards. Skiddaw's isolated position means that it is one of the most exposed ridges in Lakeland. Fortunately there are a few shelters offering refuge on the way to the trig point.

The top of **Skiddaw** is a fine viewpoint, and a description monument, commemorating the Queen's Silver Jubilee, lists the various points of interest and their distances. The fortunate will be blessed with a vivid orange sunrise over the Solway Firth. Gradually in the strengthening light appear Blencathra and the rolling Caldbeck Fells; then, more distant, the Galloway Hills and the Pennines.

Those aiming for the road-walk up Borrowdale will simply turn back here and retrace their steps to the Moot Hall. See page 52.

From the summit retrace steps southwards through the first little col and up to a sprawling shelter cairn. Now a fairly steep scree path, marked with cairns, slants down the right-hand side of the ridge. A grassy depression is reached at Carl Side Tarn (a muddy pool, not drinkable), followed by a brief rise to Carl Side's summit. The path then recommences a steep drop to some white quartzite rocks. Across the Derwent plains a wide expanse of green fields is suddenly interrupted as the north-western fells thrust sharply upwards. To the south along Borrowdale, the Scafells remain dismayingly distant. The final section of the descent is through bracken to the woods left of Benny Craig farm and so on to the Applethwaite road. Turn left along the road.

Even the following section of road can be avoided. There is little difference timewise; the field path is softer, but also wetter, underfoot. Just after the bridge of Millbeck turn right, downhill. On the left there is a house with an interesting door top motto of Latin word play. A signed field path turns off left through farm mud. At the stile at the end of the farm, slant up left to a small gate. A path leads forward on the same level through stiles and just above an adventure centre, to emerge at Applethwaite village.

The road route continues for half a mile and bears right at a small grey stone church directly into the village of Applethwaite.

At the village take a left at the telephone box where the footpath is signed to Thrushwood. (Is this where Rupert lives?) The path is slender and low sweeping nettles require some nifty footwork from the shorts wearer. Turn right along a couple of fields to reach the A591. Once across the road a path opposite leads through a field to cross the A66 Cockermouth-Penrith road for the second time today.

After crossing the road pass under a railway bridge. The indistinct path splits immediately. Our route takes the right course, rising over the field to the school. A lane goes to the right of the school then passes Crosthwaite Church. This is the parish church of Keswick, and dates back to the 15th century. The most famous incumbent was the Rev Rawnsley, one of the founder members of the National Trust.

After the crossing of the B5289, the lane opposite takes us over the river by way of a wobbly mini Severn Bridge into the village of Portinscale.

2: Borrowdale

Portinscale to Seathwaite (8 miles, 14km)

Go through the village of **Portinscale** to the T-junction just beyond the Derwentwater Hotel. Turn left along the road signposted to Grange, which passes the Derwentwater Marina. After about half a mile the road to Lake and Nichol End is reached. A wooden public footpath sign can be seen pointing into the woods of Fawe Park through a gap in the tall hedges on the left.

The right-hand path gradually rises into the woods then descends, curving right to meet a walled lane. Follow the wall until a clearing is reached. Go through the gate to the right of Lingholm following the footpath 'to Catbells'. The gardens at Lingholm are famous as the place where Beatrix Potter wrote Squirrel Nutkin. A narrow path fenced on both sides cuts through Squirrel Nutkin's woods to a second clearing. From here we can see the steep path ahead for Catbells, and to the right Rowling End and the ridge to Causey Pike are revealed.

The path re-enters the woods over a small footbridge. This path in turn leads to a kissing gate at the car park at Hawse End craft centre. A small carved bear once lived here, but on my last visit he had been cub-napped. Take the narrow road right signed 'Lake and Manesty', and pass to left of the Outdoor Centre. After about 400yds go through an iron kissing gate on the left where the path leads across a field to a pier at the edge of Derwentwater.

The pier is a good photo stop especially in the early sunlight. Morning mists hug the water's surface and cling to the many small isles on the Lake. The largest of these is St Herbert's Island. St Herbert was a 7th-century hermit, a friend and disciple of St Cuthbert of Lindisfarne. Monks sailed across the lake from Friars Crag to the island to receive blessings. The lake is quite shallow in comparison to the other lakes, averaging 18 ft (6m), with a maximum depth of 72ft (22m) near the centre. This quite often results in its freezing over completely in the winter. Over the far shore Shepherds and Gowder Crags project through oak trees on the eastern flanks of Bleaberry Fell.

Trace the shoreline path over the twisted roots of the trees to find the picnic site and tables at the Brandelhow launch pier. The

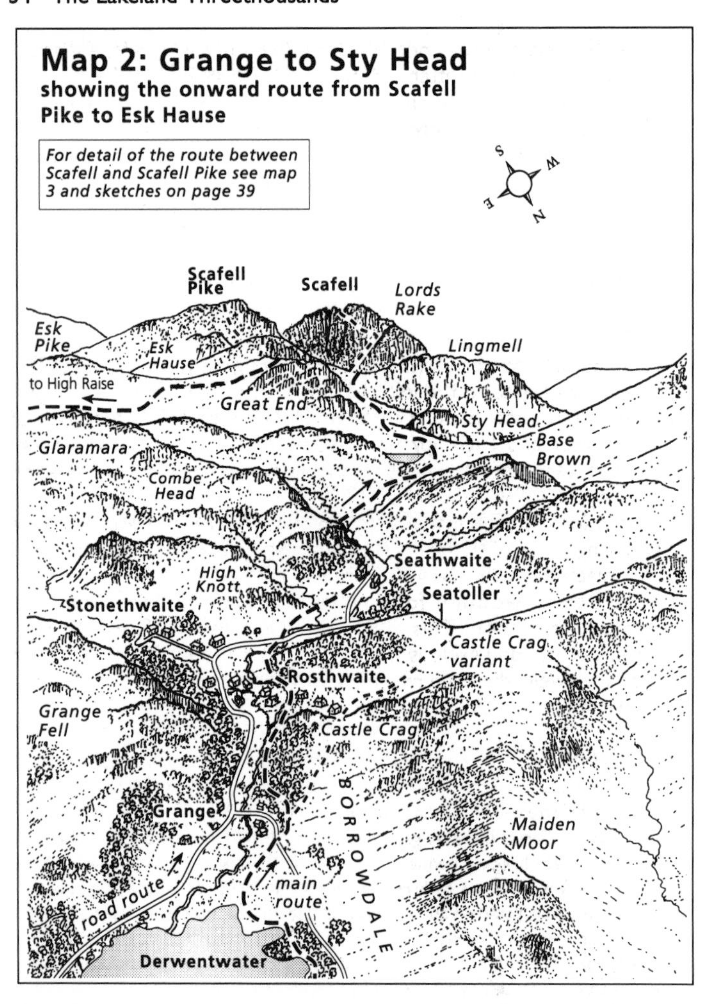

Brandelhow estate was the National Trust's first acquisition in the Lake District (1901).

Ignore the track on the right as this leads to the road too early. Instead follow the shoreline to a gate where a track goes into the woods. Go left at the 'Lodore' sign where the overhanging trees frame Abbot's Bay and Otter Island.

Go through a gate into an open field that is quite marshy in places. The worst sections are traversed by narrow wooded beams that are only wide enough for one person. A word of warning: board rage is common in the area. Before attempting to cross, it is wise to make sure that you are bigger than any person coming towards you, or you could end up waist deep in peat.

At the fourth set of boards a path to the right leads to the Grange road. This path is marked 'footpath to Lodore' in reverse. Follow it past the left-hand corner of a wood to the road. Turn left along the road for about 800yds to the Borrowdale Gates Hotel. Opposite the hotel is a public footpath rising steadily through a green pasture. The path leads to a gate to the left of a small copse. Go through the gate and turn left, soon passing through Hollows Farm. The slopes of Maiden Moor and High Spy overshadow the route with their rock-splintered escarpments falling to the red hues of the bracken-clad lower slopes.

About four hundred yards after the farm, the tarred road reaches a road triangle at the Hollows Farm campsite. Turn right, bisecting the site to reach the River Derwent (River of the Oaks).

Just after a wooden footbridge a choice of two routes to Seathwaite is offered. This alternative path behind Castle Crag is shorter, but the downside is that it involves a little more uphill. Both routes are lovely: the main route is a lovely route through more trees, this variant is lovely along the valley wall.

Castle Crag Variant: At the signpost where the path splits for Rosthwaite, take the right hand path marked 'Seatoller'. It climbs through the trees, crosses the stream on the right and traverses through the grassy hollow at the back of Castle Crag. A gate is situated at the head of the pass, after which the path begins a gentle descent. After 200yds the grass track bends uphill, but a waymarked path continues on the same level. The path heads along the valley, passing behind High Doat to reach two gates. Take the left one, again marked 'Seatoller'. This brings you onto open grass above the old coach road. Cross 50yds to the left of a pine copse onto a steep path that drops to the Honister road at the top of Seatoller.

Go through the village and turn right towards Seathwaite. If you wish to continue on the Taylorgill alternative, take a signed riverside path just before the bridge over the Derwent: otherwise continue by road to Seathwaite.

The main route follows the riverside path to the left, signed

'Rosthwaite'. After an open area the path rises and bends round to the right. Go through the second gap in the wall on the left, passing through a small quarry. The route is marked by a line of large cairns. The path turns sharply left, then returns to the river at a small pack-horse bridge. The village of Rosthwaite can be seen across the river, and behind is the Langstrath Valley and Eagle Crag.

Stay on the right hand side of the river where a narrow enclosed path brings you to the youth hostel at Longthwaite. Pass along the front of the hostel on a gravel road. The river bends to the right and the path follows with some rocky obstructions through Johnny Wood. The woods have been designated an SSSI as they are the habitat of a variety of rare algae and liverwort.

There are some chains attached to the rock to assist a safe passage where the rocks are smoothest and slippiest. In the first field after the wood, a bridge down on the left leads to a field-edge and the main Borrowdale Road. Cross the road onto a track. Keep to left of the farm and follow a waymarked path for a mile to Seathwaite.

3: The Scafells

Seathwaite to Wythburn (15 miles, 24km)

Seathwaite is the last place of civilisation for 25km, so it is useful to note that it has a telephone, toilets and a cafe beside the farm. A board at the entrance to the farm proclaims Seathwaite to be the wettest inhabit-ed place in England with average rainfall of 140 inches. Above the farm are the mines that supplied the graphite for pencil manufacturing at Keswick.

The field path from Seatoller meets the main path from the car park just to the south of the farm dwellings. A wooden direction post shows the way south-west to Sty Head. It is a wide, stony cart track following the even wider stone-choked River Derwent on its left bank. About half a mile out of Seathwaite Stockley Bridge is crossed. This neatly constructed old packhorse bridge is another good place for a photo stop. Beneath the bridge, cascading waters fill deep clear pools that are tinted by blue-grey rocks.

The walker is now encircled by wild fells and rugged crags: to the left Hind Crag, ahead Seathwaite Fell and to the south-west, the deep ravine of Taylorgill and the crags at the foot of Base Brown. The path ascends to a gate and continues to rise rapidly to the left of a fence, weaving a course between rocky slabs. Follow the fence above the falls to reach a giant boulder at the 1000ft (305m) contour. This height has been helpfully etched into the boulder. The gradient then becomes less acute as we enter the valley of Sty Head. The path is erratic in this area as it follows the left side of the stream until it reaches a footbridge (GR 224102), which should be crossed.

The Taylor Gill Variant: The path to Sty Head from Seathwaite is one many have trodden before. An interesting alternative exists on the west side of the valley. This is the same length as the main route, but rougher.

At Seathwaite farm, turn right, between the farm buildings. After a few yards turn left through an arch, and pass the campsite to a footbridge over the River Derwent. A gate on the left leads to a rough path that passes upstream and below a pine plantation. The path then slants up right, away from the stream, to a ladder stile at the top corner of a second plantation.

Continue through rocky ground slightly uphill towards the base of the crags. The path, now clear again, goes through a gate on a ledge terrace. There is a fine view of Taylorgill Force from beneath the overhanging rocks. Just above the gate is a short, easy scramble; then the path crosses the top of a scree and passes above the top of the waterfall. The small path continues, to right of the stream, and rejoins the main route at the footbridge.

After a further half-mile you reach **Sty Head Tarn** and Sty Head Pass – the name means 'Top of the Ladder'. It is common to see a multitude of brightly-coloured tents here.

The route from the tarn can be difficult to find in mist. The path, pitched in parts, passes to the right of the tarn. Just before the first aid box take a bearing of 165 degrees, crossing the marshy bowl to the right side of a spur and descending for a minute or two towards Wasdale. After losing about 20m of height, contour left below a small crag, to find the beginning of the clear path raking across the flank of Great End. The **Corridor Route**, formerly known as the Guides' Route, crosses three spectacular ravines before reaching Lingmell Col. The first is Skew Gill, where the path dips into the gill and climbs out onto reddish stone. The second, Greta Gill, is quite tricky, but arrows are scratched into the rock showing the way over some slabs. There are some waterfalls in the gill just below the path. It is from here that the best photographs of the sharks-back shape of Lingmell with the most spectacular of gorges, Piers Gill, can be taken.

Just short of the 700m level a small tarn is passed, after which the path splits (GR215079). The left path ascends Scafell Pike in a stony gully, but we want the small path on the right. This goes around a grassy hump and crosses the top of Piers Gill to follow a wall up to

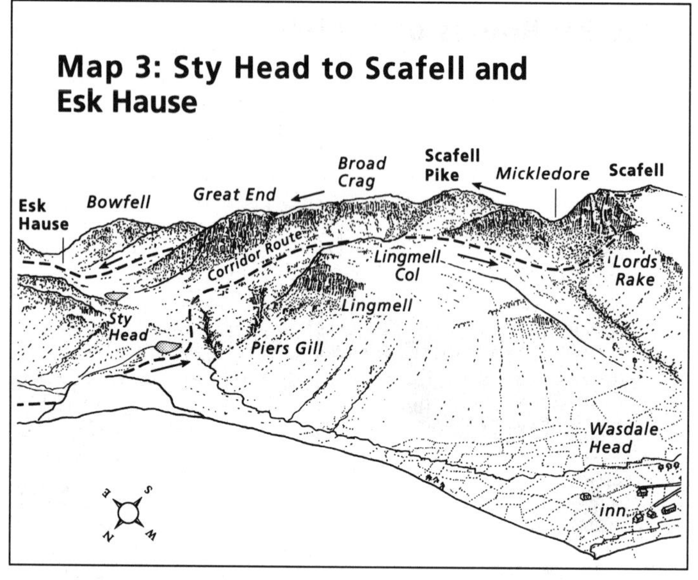

the **Lingmell Col**.

The immediate focus is the magnificent Wastwater amid a mosaic of green fields, a vision marred only by the white plumes of steam from the nuclear plant at Sellafield. Fortunately the rock scenery of Scafell more than compensates for this eyesore.

Go straight through the col, joining a wide path coming down from the left. A narrow trail traversing the boulders can be found to the left along the foot of Pikes Crag. Some of England's finest rock climbs including Scafell Pinnacle, Central Buttress and Moss Gill can be viewed from here. The path has some small scattered cairns and is fairly easy to trace. But if it is lost, then drop to gentler grassy slopes below the stonefields, and climb again on reaching the large pitched path ascending out of Wasdale to **Hollow Stones**.

From a three-metre boulder on the floor of the hollow, continue up the path for 40yds, and then turn right to go up the left edge of a scree fan into the heart of the crag face above. It has been some time since we achieved our last threethousander and the steep slippery screes of Scafell provide a frustrating obstacle. For every two steps forward, you slide one step backwards. At 700m you reach a rock

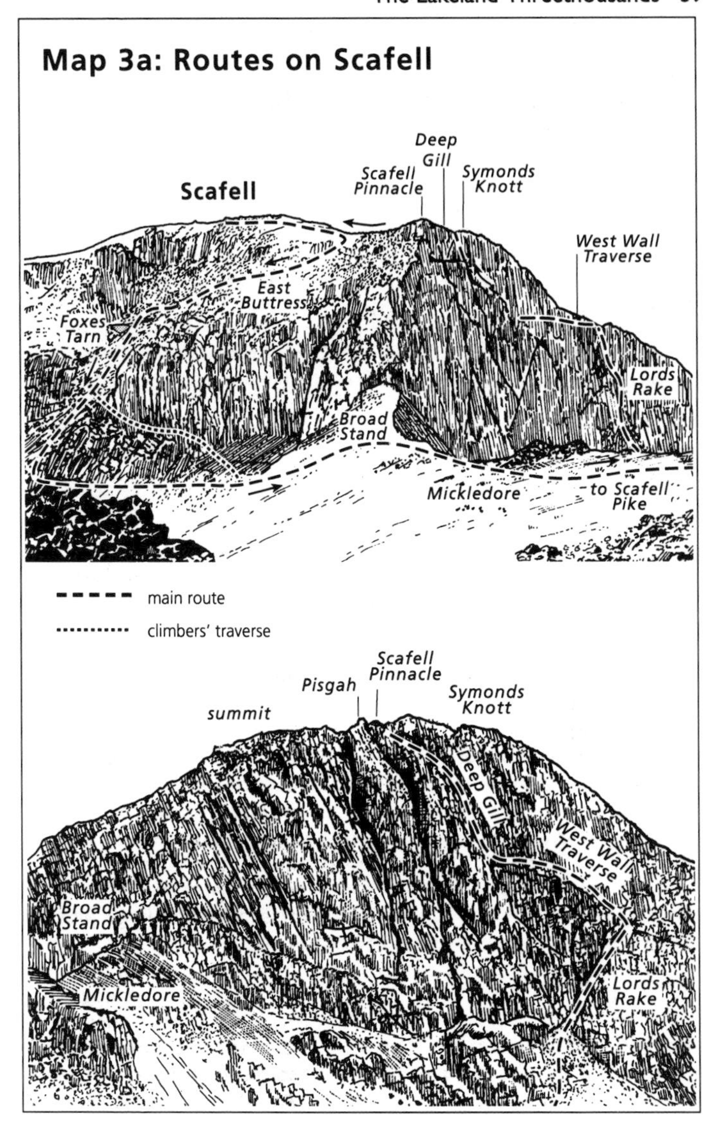
Map 3a: Routes on Scafell
Scafell
Deep Gill
Scafell Pinnacle
Symonds Knott
West Wall Traverse
East Buttress
Foxes Tarn
Lords Rake
Broad Stand
Mickledore
to Scafell Pike
main route
climbers' traverse
Scafell Pinnacle
Pisgah
summit
Symonds Knott
Deep Gill
West Wall Traverse
Broad Stand
Mickledore
Lords Rake

wall, heralding the start of **Lords Rake**, a seemingly vertical gully requiring the use of hands. Turn right into the Rake. The best strategy is to alternate sides to find the firmest footing. The centre is quite loose and stones are easily disturbed. If a rock should be dislodged it is customary to shout "below!" and apologise to the walker behind you. However this does not apply when the falling object is yourself. In such circumstances best stay quiet and allow the poor unfortunate to provide you with a soft landing – then apologise.

The Rake all the Way variant: The spectacular West Wall Traverse, just ahead, involves an even steeper and looser gully. If you don't fancy that, then there is an easier route that reaches the top of Scafell by following Lords Rake to its end. At the top of the gully go straight ahead, passing behind a pinnacle. Descend with sheer rock on the left, and climb to pass behind a second pinnacle. After another brief descent, the path traverses to a scree and goes up onto the west ridge of Scafell. Go up this for ten minutes to the plateau, and turn right for 200yds to the summit of Scafell.

About ten yards before the top of the steep gully a gritty groove angles back on the left and begins a stony path across the face. The formidable crag of Central Buttress towers ahead – looking outwards, the sunny face of Gable and even the stonefields of Scafell Pike seem like a different and friendlier world. The path ends at a second steep loose gully.

The dark chasm of Deep Gill is one of my favourite places in all of England. Dark, wet rock walls tower above the walker, instilling a sense of vulnerability. The gully narrows and steepens near the top and I challenge you not to use your hands on the last bit. The way splits in the last few yards and the left exit is best, being less gritty. Both exits tend to be covered in ice in winter and can be treacherous.

The plateau is reached quite unexpectedly. Now on firm ground, look out between the rocky pinnacles and down the Gill – the expressions of ascending walkers can prove entertaining. Head directly away from the edge to find Scafell's summit a few minutes away across the stony plateau. There is a small circular shelter next to the cairn.

Scafell

There is a magnificent vista from the top obscured only northwards by the bulk of Scafell Pike. Southwards are Morecambe Bay and

Furness, with Burnmoor Tarn in the foreground. To the East Bowfell and the Crinkle Crags are separated from Scafell by the deep barren divide of Upper Eskdale. Looking west, the pastel greens and reds of Mosedale intermingle at the foot of Pillar.

The quickest route down into Mickledore by Broad Stand is described on page 43. To descend the West Wall Traverse is an option, but risks kicking stones onto those coming up. The best route is by Foxes Tarn.

Descent from Scafell by Foxes Tarn: The path to Foxes Tarn retraces steps towards Deep Gill, but, in the dip just before the crag-tops, branches down right at a cairn. This path, that drops down steep scree to Foxes Tarn, is the oldest pitched path in the Lake District. The tarn itself, in its hollow at 820m, is the second highest named pool of water in Lakeland and also the smallest, although it was almost obliterated in the late 1950s when storms sent rocks and debris crashing down the slopes of Scafell.

A huge boulder lies plonked in the middle of the crescent shaped waters. The path stays left of the tarn and follows the outflow stream.

Roy approaches Lingmell on his third attempt Photo: James Clayton

After three minutes of descent, the stream bends right while the path continues ahead to the top of a narrow rock-filled gully.

The Climbers' Traverse: this narrow and spectacular path saves 200ft (60m) of descent. It is not recommended in windy or icy conditions. It is not easy to find the start and if you set out across the slope at the wrong point you will find yourself among vertical crags: return and follow the main route down the gully.

About 20ft (6m) above the top of the boulder gully, leave the path and scramble up a short rock groove on the left. (A 2ft perched boulder is just to the right of the groove top). Traverse horizontally across a scree to a rock-and-grass groove that slants up below a rock wall to a cairn. After this awkward bit the path becomes clear, along the base of vertical rocks. It descends to the screes below Mickledore. Turn left below the overhanging crags to climb to the pass.

The alternative to the Climbers' Traverse is to descend another 200ft (60m) down the rock-filled gully to meet the path from Eskdale. From the foot of the gully turn left up the loose path which is a cocktail of pink, grey and white stones in the midst of the white boulders. The easiest going is to stay below the left-hand crags right up to the ridge

Scafell Pike from the top of Deep Gill on Scafell

of Mickledore. There is a first aid box at the Scafell-Pike end of the narrow ridge.

Descent From Scafell By Broad Stand: The most infamous descent from Scafell is Broad Stand: a rock climb graded moderate. John Parker, author of 'Cumbria', suggests that the route requires a blind grope, a little faith and some contortions. It is not a place for the inexperienced and many have come to grief here.

From the summit cairn, return north-east to reach the northern cliffs at the top of Deep Gill. Turn right alongside the clifftop, passing Scafell Pinnacle. Start the descent at a small cairn, 40yds in from the cliff edge. Scramble down to a small rock gully, and go down the rim of this, immediately to its left, on scratched rocks, to reach a wide scree shelf above Mickledore. You are now 30ft (10m vertical) above Mickledore, and 50yds sideways.

A sprawling cairn marks the top of a 6ft (2m) groove. At the bottom is a rock spike belay. Now a slightly overhanging wall leads down to a triangular shelf. There are two ways down the wall. Holds on the right-hand (outer) edge are good, but seriously exposed. At the inner (left-hand) edge the holds are not as good, but still serviceable.

The rest of the descent is easier. Go down the sloping shelf and round to the top of a narrow chimney behind a protruding bit. Wriggle down the chimney known as 'Fat Man's Agony'. Finally step down to the red pebbles of Mickledore.

The final climb to Scafell Pike is tedious and not easy, although playing dot to dot with the cairns should eventually lead the tired traveller to the top. Many find their own route clambering over the huge jammed boulders. Not all the boulders are jammed, some move just to keep you on your toes, or even put you on your nose, before falling back into place with a clunk.

Scafell Pike

It will have felt like an eternity to claim peak number two, but only one now remains. While you may feel you deserve the rest there is little time to savour the view, even if you have one to savour. There are always too many people on the top and at least one dog eager to help with your lunch. Besides, you're not supposed to be enjoying this.

Leave the summit initially towards Bowfell (east) and then curving NNE to find the path. This descends over a tricky rock section to the depression before Broad Crag. It is satisfying to know the depression is worse for those coming the other way to Scafell Pike. The path rises steeply to the right of Broad Crag then levels out over its bouldered

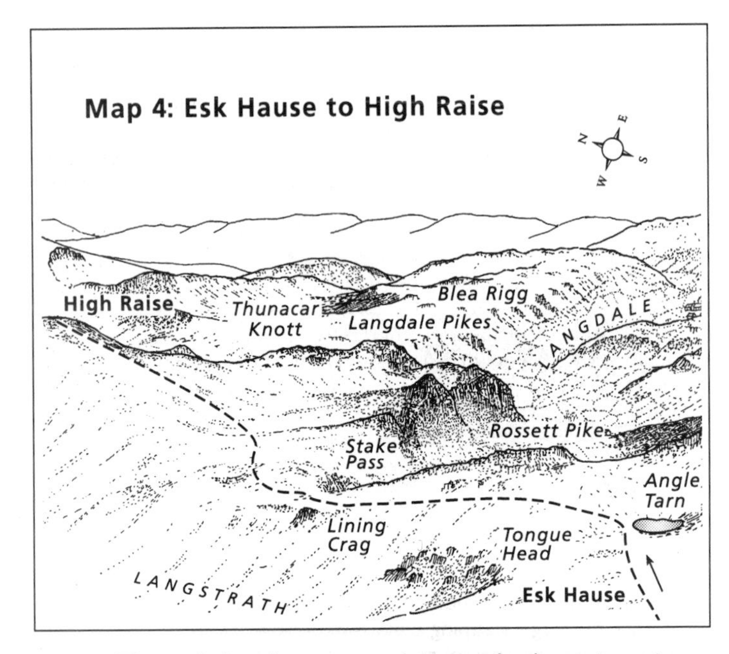

summit. The track then drops a second time to the depression prior to Ill Crag. The path this time passes to the left of the main top and passes a long line of cairns. Great End has now come into view ahead and there are good views of Borrowdale and Derwentwater.

The path to Esk Hause is well worn and starts as a loose shale descent around the right-hand flank of Great End. There is a valuable stream here. **Esk Hause**, at 750m, is the highest pass in England and the crossroads of the Lake District. The proliferation of paths makes the area confusing in mist. At the first col branch left, and go down for 300yds (about 3 minutes) to a welcoming cross-shaped shelter. Turn right onto a descending pitched path.

The terrain is now slowly transforming from arid rocks to wild grass and peat. The wide and badly worn path crosses a double depression. The final descent to Angle Tarn is again constructed of pitched boulders. The waters of this tarn change colour with the moods of Bowfell, whose northern facade of Hanging Knott is reflected on its surface. To left is the long deep hollow of Langstrath – a

Roy at Angle Tarn, beneath Bowfell

side-branch of Borrowdale.

Cross the large stepping stones at the outflow of Angle Tarn and follow the erosion control signs to the left. The path climbs for a few steps and then splits. The path to Stake Pass contours left on a bearing of 290 degrees. It peters out in boggy ground after 3/4 mile (1km), but can be regained by slanting right, uphill. Or the ridgeline above can be followed down into the Stake Pass.

Here consult your watch. Two hours of daylight are required to reach Wythburn Church – the Wythburn valley in the dark is quite horrific. The path to the left, into Langstrath, is the last safe escape, and leads back into Borrowdale.

After crossing the head of **Stake Pass** near a tarn, keep straight ahead across hummocky ground at the head of Stake Beck. The gooiest bits of path have white stones embedded in the peat making an interesting colour contrast as well as a useful survival aid.

The next stage is a tough ascent of 1000ft (300m) over the spongy grass on the west of **High Raise**. Paths here are less obvious than most maps suggest. The area is also littered with small ankle-twisting holes that pose a danger to the tired walker. After crossing several small veins of water the broad ridge is reached and the 2500ft summit, marked by a trig point, is to the left.

Helvellyn, the last of the three thousanders, is now clearly visible above the forest line. Sadly, it still seems to be rather a long way away.

From here a last escape to Borrowdale is possible by following the broad path northwards to the col of Greenup Edge and then bearing left. The path after the col is faint to follow, especially in fading light. It must be followed carefully, as high Lining Crag is below it on the left.

Strike off the summit ENE down grassy slopes, beneath which a path runs to the right. Just before this path starts climbing towards the low pass to Easedale, turn off left on a smaller path, which circles round the right-hand edge of the Wythburn bog-bowl. It flattens at a marshy area unflatteringly known as 'the Bog'; the path is intermittent, remaining always on the right side. After a couple of miles the valley steepens and there are some pleasant waterfalls surrounded by rowan trees. Continue along the right bank of the stream, ignoring the foot-bridge on the left, to cross a couple of ladder stiles. After the second one, turn back sharply right and cross another at the corner of a wood. A stony track leads to West Head Farm (named 'Steel End' on maps) and then to the Armboth road.

Turn right and follow this for a few minutes to reach the busy A591. Directly opposite, a footpath in the woods just above the road leads quickly down to the car park at **Wythburn Church**.

4: Helvellyn

Wythburn to Keswick (11 miles 18km)

At Wythburn is a phone box that can be used to summon friends or taxi-drivers. However, given clear windless weather and good torches, confident walkers can reasonably attempt Helvellyn despite the onset of darkness. The paths up the mountain are wide and easy, though the descent will be rough and very tiresome.

On a recent visit to Helvellyn I had to explain to the bus driver where Wythburn was. Today Wythburn is nothing more than a white larch-surrounded church and a few scattered cottages. However in the last century the village was a favourite spot of the Lakeland poets Wordsworth and Coleridge. The lake of Leathes Water occupied the site with the villages of Armboth and Wythburn at its north and south

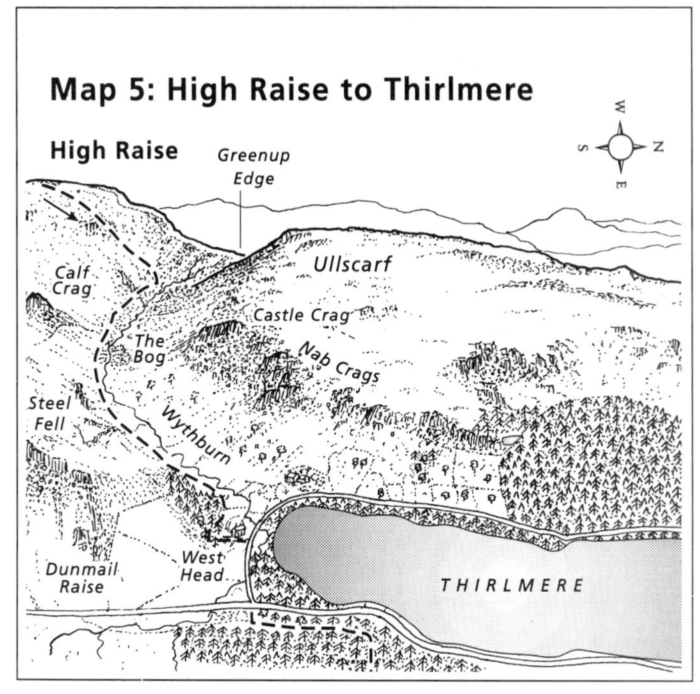

ends respectively. In 1894 the villages were flooded with nine billion gallons of water to form the Thirlmere Reservoir, which supplies most of Manchester's water. The church, constructed in 1640, rebuilt a hundred years later and further extended in 1872, survived as a result of its elevated position.

The path to Helvellyn begins at the second car park immediately behind the churchyard. Go through the wooden kissing gate and turn right to the tree-cloaked slopes on the west of Helvellyn. The trees, predominantly Norwegian spruce, were planted to firm the ground and prevent debris slipping into the Thirlmere Reservoir.

This is a steep ascent on a comfortable bed of pine needles lasting for about a half mile. At the halfway point the route is crossed by a forestry track. Go over the stile or (if very tired) through the dog flap and continue climbing steeply. At the end of the forest a five bar gate and stile are found. Erosion control fences force you to zig-zag onto the open fell beneath Comb Crag. After all the zigging and zagging the path heads north-east towards Whelpside Gill. The Gill is particularly striking from here as its streams (the highest water source in the Lakes) transform into a raging torrent down the Helvellyn massif. As height is gained there are good views of Thirlmere, Ullscarf, Harrop Tarn and the Wythburn valley.

On achieving the top of the ridge the path turns left over a boggy area before resuming a gentler ascent to the west of Nethermost Pike. After a mile or so the path comes to a col, where it joins a track from Dollywaggon and Nethermost Pikes.

Near Helvellyn's summit, a stone commemorates the landing of an aeroplane on the summit in 1926. The summit itself has a cross-shaped shelter – probably the most visited in the Lake District – and an OS column just beyond.

Helvellyn

From the top the best vantage is to the east. Red Tarn lies 275m below hemmed in by two spectacular ridges: Striding Edge and the less climbed Swirral Edge. Beyond, the twisting blue waters of Ullswater lead the eye to the Pennines. This is also a last opportunity to look back to Scafell Pike, Scafell and Skiddaw. All the threethousands have now been conquered.

Leave Helvellyn on a bearing of 310 degrees (north-west), passing the top of Swirral Edge. The broad track skirts just left of the slight rise of Lower Man, then heads (still north-west) down a broad flat ridge. Browncove Crag drops steeply on the right. At the ridge end the stony track steepens. Now a pitched path, it twists and turns as wooden fences control the direction of descent.

At the 300m contour the path meets a walled plantation and turns northwards. Cross over a wooden footbridge where there is a wooden signpost to Sticks Pass and Stanah. The main road, and Thirlmere, are not far below. Raven Crag is prominent on the far shore at the head of the lake.

The path goes on the right hand side of a wall. It is narrow, but less rocky than the descent from Helvellyn. The waymarked path soon leaves the wall and rises about ten metres above it remaining parallel to the road. The track drops back down to the wall where the Kings Head pub can be seen through a gap in the wall.

The landlord of the pub was once charged with responsibility for painting the stones on the White Stones track to Helvellyn. Resist the temptation for a sharp exit – it is too early for that celebratory pint.

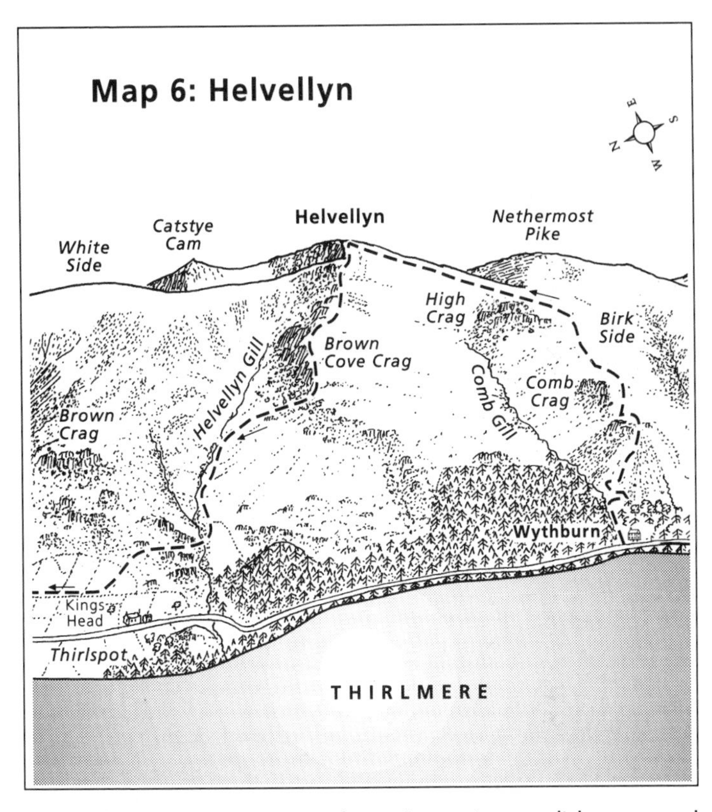

The path continues over rugged terrain passing wet lichen-covered rocks and bracken slopes. Interest is maintained by the fine vantage of St John's Vale with Blencathra, and some impressive waterfalls at Fisher Place. Go straight on at a junction of paths.

On reaching a rocky glen at **Stanah** cross the footbridge and descend sharply towards the Keswick road, passing the back of the farm at Stybeck. A stone plaque points right, through a gate to a stone step-stile. The path then follows the course of the aqueduct. Go through the gate to the left of the farm which brings you to a minor road. Go left to the phone box, passing a caravan site. Turn right along the vale road, passing Legburnthwaite youth hostel. About two

On the route down Helvellyn, with Skiddaw on the horizon

hundred yards along the road a public footpath crosses a field on the left to reach the A591.

Those caught by darkness now have little choice but to return to Keswick along the main road. For those with daylight to do it in, the footpath route is much nicer, but, unfortunately, a half-mile longer.

Turn right along the road where there is a narrow footpath on the east side. After about 400yds a bus shelter and a dual carriageway sign are passed. On the east side of the road a public footpath is marked 'St Johns in the Vale Church and Bridge House'. The path enters the woods. Follow the yellow markers, at the first fork taking the right turning, then the left fork shortly after. The walk then becomes a terrace about 50ft (15m) above the river. To the left steep rock and tree clad slopes restrict the view, but east is the high rough ridge from the Dodds to Clough Head. The Castle Rock of Triermain protrudes from the midst of the pines. Those that do not already climb could be tempted to start at the sight of this spectacular pillar of rock.

The path dips to a wall and follows the riverbank. After a further half-mile (3/4km) the track passes to the left of Low Bridge End farm where afternoon teas are an option. Such a leisurely idea does not seem fitting with the day's pace. Perhaps evening teas would be more appropriate.

At the far end of the farm a side-path splits off right towards Sosgill Bridge – but the simpler continuation is to follow the more prominent

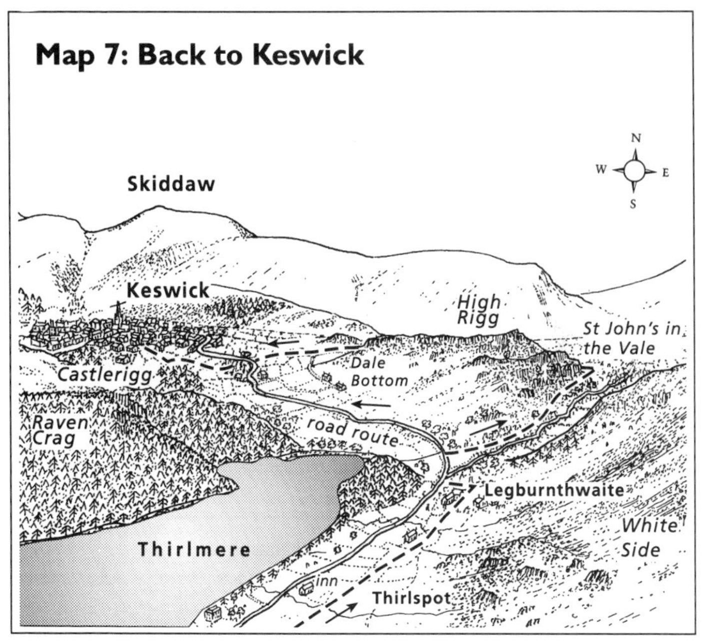

path straight ahead as it pokes in and out of the woods following the wall.

Blencathra and the village of Threlkeld come into view to the north. Threlkeld was once an important lead mining and quarrying town. Many of the streets of northern England were paved with granite from here. Telegraph wires prevent the photographer from getting an otherwise perfectly framed photo of Blencathra's fine gullies and ridges.

The path begins a sharp rise as it nears the church of St John's in the Vale. At the small church and youth centre turn left along the road. After a gate a gravel farm road descends towards Skyes farm. The evening sun casts shadows across the North-western Fells that have now come into the picture. Where the road bends to the left a public footpath sign ahead shows the way through a field via a kissing gate. Negotiate a route around the rocky slabs that intersperse the field and find another kissing gate. Make a dog-leg through the middle of a field where a solitary signpost is marked for Keswick. Cross a footbridge and a couple of muddy fields, to rise to the main road through a gap in a wall.

Turn right to the top of the hill about 100yds away. Road walking to Keswick can be avoided by following the path marked 'Walla Crag' on the west side of the road. From this field there is a fine prospect of the whole upper Helvellyn ridge.

At the top of the field is a ladder stile, and here the path goes right. The farm of Rakefoot is two hundred yards away on the left as the path descends slightly to a lane. Turn left for 25yds, then right to drop into a small glen. Cross the stream and turn right along the wooded banks. This is signed 'Keswick via Great Wood'.

Derwentwater suddenly comes into sight, but an ugly radio mast mars the view. The path descends into woods. Do not cross the bridge, but remain on the left bank of the beck as Spring farm is approached. The church spire can be seen above white-washed cottages and Bassenthwaite Lake. Go past a farm to reach Ambleside Road on the edge of Keswick.

Turn left towards the town centre. The street takes you directly to the Moot Hall.

Road Alternatives

1: Borrowdale

It's much better to use the off-road route round the back of Derwentwater. That said, the Borrowdale road is not unpleasant as road-walks go. Though no shorter, it is easier than the main route and saves about half an hour.

From Skiddaw summit, return down the ridge southwards for 600yds until it steepens. Here the path is, in the dark, invisible. Turn south-east to descend scree and rediscover it. Return to the Moot Hall in Keswick.

Turn right in the Market Square, passing the Dog and Gun pub. The path passes the church to reach a mini roundabout. Go straight ahead along the B5289 Borrowdale road. Paths start straight away on the right behind a tall hedge and run in and out of the woods among slender trees.

The paths run between the road and the lake, to emerge at Barrow House youth hostel. This was formerly a guest house run by Bob Graham; and here, on a summer morning in 1932, you could have been served breakfast by a bleary-eyed host who had spent the previous 24 hours running over 42 Lakeland peaks.

After a short section of road, a path on the left slants into the wood (signposted 'Rejoins Road'). Leave it for a permissive path (marked by white arrows) that runs behind the Lodore Hotel. A short diversion can be taken to visit the Lodore waterfalls before rejoining the road through the hotel yard.

After Lodore there are no more paths beside the road. It is much nicer, and really just as quick, to turn right over the double-arched bridge into Grange, turn left in the village to Hollows Farm camp-site, and rejoin our main off-road paths.

If ignoring that advice and remaining relentlessly roadbound, do still take the slight short-cut on the left that passes the Bowder Stone, a 36ft tall boulder weighing over two thousand tons. Apart from this it is road and verge all the way to Strands Bridge, just short of Seatoller (where you turn left onto the Allerdale Ramble path).

2: Helvellyn to Keswick

If night has fallen you'll have to take the six miles of road from Swirls car park to Keswick. Among the road's unpleasant features are the white painted milestones that are illuminated by passing traffic and are a reminder of just how far is left to go. Looking on the bright side, the main A591 carries little traffic at night.

After Causeway Foot there is a pavement on the left hand side of the road, and at the top of Nest Brow the orange lights of Keswick

Roy and Boyen taking a well-earned rest at Derwentwater

reappear suddenly. After a cruel 1 in 3 descent you reach the town. The street signposted 'Keswick via Manor Brow' saves a half-mile, and runs straight to the Moot Hall.

THE LONGEST SHORTEST DAY

A midwinter attempt on the Threethousands

As a run for the 21st December, the Lakes Threethousands is just the thing. Skiddaw is easy to do in the dark, and so is the little road up Borrowdale. A 2:00 am start thus gets you to Stonethwaite with almost nine hours of daylight and half-light to play around in. To make things even easier, nice crisp snow covers the boulderfields of Scafell Pike like icing on the Christmas cake, while the rubble of Lord's Rake gets conveniently frozen solid.

At the solstice of 1997, though, the boulders were covered in raindrops, not snow (and any pastry cook will tell you that a Christmas cake left out in the rain does not become any easier to walk across). And our two-in-the-morning start had lazily declined into quarter past five. Well, Joss Naylor did the Threes in eight and a half hours so we should manage thirteen; and the paths over Helvellyn are nice wide ones that show up in the dark. Meanwhile, the weather forecast offered nothing more interestingly wintry than boggy patches on Helvellyn.

Skiddaw was indeed not difficult, though it did puzzle us slightly when the very plain path disappeared altogether at the grassy col above Latrigg. It's mist and darkness together that make things tricky; the torch shows only glare, and has to be held at knee-level. But as the track steepened it became stony and climbed out of the mist. Shapes of hill showed between cloud below and cloud above, but the real vision was Keswick. A thin mist drifted above Keswick, so that it shone through a plasma of electric orange to make a picture of the Birth of Streetlights out of the Primordial Neon Cloud.

Above, the half-moon showed through holes in the clouds. We didn't need torches to follow the path around the high side of Little Man, above the black hole of Skiddaw Forest. Skiddaw mountain is cold and stony, but it doesn't take long to touch the trig and turn back. The cloud dropped a few metres and swallowed up the ridge. It was a thin cloud and the moonlight crept through to show the stones – to show also the ridgeline as it bent away left.

Left? Surely that ridgeline should be straight. The compass agreed: that wasn't south at all. The stone slope got steeper than it should, we bent right to look for south and wondered whether to start fiddling with torches and maps. But bright Keswick reappeared, so we didn't have to. Yes, wide and obvious paths do vanish mysteriously into the night. And yes: the ridgeline does bend left. The lesson was not lost on us. If it should happen to get dark with us still on Helvellyn, we wouldn't just use the compass – we'd use the map as well.

Back at the Moot Hall it was eight o' clock and broad daylight. This meant we could take the woodland path alongside the Borrowdale road, the path with the rocks and the tree roots and the views of the Derwentwater island. The Derwentwater island was to be the last view of that long day – though the camera didn't agree about the broad daylight and asked for a full second of exposure.

After Grange there are no more rocks and tree roots but only road, so we crossed the long double-arch bridge where they drowned the witch in *Rogue Herries*, and went on through the empty campsite and the grey leafless trees on the wrong side of the river.

The sheepdogs of Borrowdale are a race apart – their legs are long, their coats are short, and their ears are an unusual shape. The man behind the dogs offered the mildest of warnings: "you're not going to see much up there." The camera had not been lying: the clouds above were getting blacker, and also less far above. And somehow, the long ascent to Lingmell seemed even longer than it should. But Borrowdale was the problem. We'd cleverly managed to avoid the road, but nothing can eliminate the flatness of the valley bottom, and flatness means running. As any walker can tell you, running is tiring. The sensible way would have been to incorporate some restful uphills into that part of the journey: Catbells, perhaps, or Great Gable. Eight miles of flatlanding has led us into ignoble flatland attitudes, so that three thousand feet of climb seems a task rather than a treat, and we reach Hollow Stones at noon when it should really have been ten in the morning.

However, at Hollow Stones it starts to take on Atmosphere. What's the point of Winter if you don't get Atmosphere? The bottom rocks of the screeshoot poke towards us out of the cloud, and at the top of the screeshoot the gully walls are black and dripping. We wonder about the West Wall Traverse: Glyn is no scrambler. However, Glyn has come down Lord's Rake escorting Bob Graham runners too timid for Broad Stand – and the West Wall Traverse isn't a scramble so much as a spectacular place among crags and another stony gully.

The spectacular place isn't among crags but among mist – but still spectacular, even if I do have to talk Glyn through the view and explain that Mickledore is just down and out there. The view from the West

Wall is just as good when it's invisible. The grey rock may seep up into black shadow, but that black shadow goes on up for hundreds of feet. And it's not just me saying, as the drips from out of the mist corroborate.

The spectacular place is still spectacular – but the stony gully is no longer entirely stony. Wet, greyish ice blocks it: ice, the very colour, texture and temperature of our hillrunning feet.

To climb round on the loose gully wall could be to head up into a dead end, for there may be more obstructing ice above, and loose walls are much harder to do downwards. But we haven't been excited since the orange spider web above misted Keswick, and the day is basically warm not icy. So we make our crumbling way above the icy bit and, indeed, find no further ice. Though the summit plateau is a lot colder than the enclosures of the icy gully.

We hop around the rocks with our compasses out, and find the summit and the descent towards Foxes Tarn. This steep slope of scree and stone boasts the first-ever pitched path since the ones built by miners for ponies. Twenty years on, the path is well blended in. You look at the jammed stones, and realise that at a particular point the jamming is slightly less random, and that what you're looking at is a path that twists steeply down, sometimes zig-zagging in turns tighter than its own width. It's not an easy path, but likable, and it drops quick and hard to a very likable place.

We allow ourselves a moment of rest at Foxes Tarn. I have replaced the customary sugar-rich apple tartlets with the mince pies of the season – but Glyn's stomach isn't up to anything so adventurous. Foxes' Tarn is good on a good day. In mist, its little lawn and its shelter are even more enjoyable; and its large rock at the middle of a very small pool is designed for close-up viewing when mist blanks out the distracting precipices of Scafell and Eskdale. Two mince pies and tarn water – a moment of comfort in a cruel world.

Glyn seems pleased with the Climbers' Traverse: "a good place," he murmurs, "another good place;" and it's not just because it's saving us two hundred feet of descent into Eskdale. For again we feel rather than see the huge misted crags above, the wide spaces below the right-hand shoe. Again, there are exciting lumps of ice. For the benefit of the non-scrambler behind, I demonstrate a subtle but safe press-hold below the rim of the iced-over path. But the non-scrambler simply steps across.

Great lumps of water splat onto the scree from the overhangs alongside Mickledore. We linger for a moment to take in some more Atmosphere. This particular Atmosphere is arriving in large wet lumps from the direction of Wasdale Head. It seems a long way up Scafell Pike, considering the smallness and insignificance of that hill alongside its greater neighbour. Not unexpectedly, we have England's high point to ourselves. Similarly, our fellow hill lovers have respected our privacy over the wet boulders of Ill Crag and Great End.

At last, we can do some of this running we're so keen on. It has been a peculiarly cruel expedition: running with not a step to walk from Skiddaw's trig to Seathwaite Head, then walking with not a step to run, all the way up Scafell and then over the exciting places, the screes and the boulders. But now it's a more familiar rhythm of trot, stride and hop across a bog. A red jacket appears in the gloom ahead. Has the red jacket been on the Pike? It has – but not Scafell. We have been, it would seem, the only ones with the particular inspiration to do Scafell today.

"Where are you off to, then?" the red jacket wants to know. Glyn is embarrassed, but I believe in promoting mutual understanding between runners and walkers, so let the word 'Helvellyn' drift back on tendrils of mist. The long grass to High Raise goes shorter in running shoes, specially as we're cleverly going for Sergeant Man instead. We find the col – and that was tricky slantwise work, balancing the fall line against the compass-bearing. We find, eventually, the rock-knoll that's Sergeant Man, although only after finding several of the rock-knolls that aren't. However, night falls about an hour before we really want it to.

The map calls it, simply, The Bog – as if there were no other, as if the forecast hadn't promised us something along those lines on the Helvellyn ridge. Going to the Bog: this phrase neatly expresses Wyth Burn in the dark, in the wet, at the end of a wet Autumn. The semi-solid wastes of five hills trickle into this cleft in the moor, putrefy for a while, and then, eventually, trickle out again.

The path is down among the tussocks, well hidden from the questing torch, so the way is to follow the stream. But the stream isn't actually going anywhere itself. We hear it trickling over on the left, try to walk away from it, and find it suddenly at our toes in the misted torchlight. The ground itself feels shaky and insecure, but that's just the effect of dark, disorientation and being a bit tired.

Well, that's what it is until Glyn's leg goes through and we realise that it is, in fact, quaking bog. "I'm afraid you'll have to pull me out," says Glyn, and I realise with alarm that he's gone all taut and British, like the man in the quicksand in *Lawrence of Arabia* – and also that I, being at this point rather lighter and brisker, am six steps further forward across the same stuff. I tiptoe back, and extract him with a quick

Thirlmere from the slopes of Helvellyn with Skiddaw on the horizon

tug on the rucksack strap.

But where is firm ground? This valley cleft could be open moor for all we can see in six feet of glaring torchlight, but it was once a lake. Has that lake really drained away, or does its ghost still lie, uneasy, in its former bed? Is it just below the turf, temporarily buried in a shallow grave? Everything wobbles a bit, when stood on by one who's started to think about Grimpen Mire. Did the last set of figures from the Wasdale Mountain Rescue include any morass accidents?

We step delicately out to the valley side, and find a little boggy path. And when we get to the main road, the afternoon bus whizzes by, all lit up and cheerful. And it's still only six o' clock.

The only reason not to go on up Helvellyn is that someone might see our lights and call the Rescue. But the mist will cover our lights.

So we go on up Helvellyn. We go on up Helvellyn quite quickly, considering that we do have to spend a bit of time hunting down, in the misted darkness, the wide and obvious path. Sudden wind on the right ear indicates our arrival on the summit ridge; a corner of the stone shelter pokes into the torchlight and indicates the summit itself. These conditions do emphasise the resemblance of this structure to an urban bus shelter – but the brisk wind has carried away the litter and most of the distinctive bus-shelter smell. Glyn thinks he could manage a mince pie.

Down off Helvellyn was an interesting exercise in mountain minimalism. We decided on something called the 'Old Pony Route', as this seemed to have no nasty steep stuff till right at the bottom. We put in fresh batteries. The fresh batteries allowed us to see rather more mist than we could before, and we passed an interesting quarter of an hour steering around what looked like a small shadowed dip in the ground but was in fact the thousand-foot east face of the mountain.

According to the map, this pony path has no top, so we stayed on the ridge, then slanted down grassy slopes to pounce on it from above. A path with no top to it isn't going to be a popular path in these degenerate peak-bagging times. The Old Pony Route exists, but only just. It is certainly much less there than paths we'd had no trouble loosing earlier in the trip.

However, the human eye is particularly skilled at recognising patterns – even patterns so faint they're almost not there at all. Thus we have astrology, the canals of Mars, and the Old Pony Route off Helvellyn. Eye thought it was beginning to get the hang of it, offered to feet a tentative program for detecting invisible paths. Brain was now in a trance-like sleep state and not butting in with 'come off it, a non-existent path by torchlight in the mist'; so Eye and Foot, left to get on with it, followed the Old Pony Route right down to Thirlspot. And a nice path it was too: small and grassy, soft but not boggy, and not too steep for well walked-on feet – except for the nasty bit at the bottom when the torch batteries had finally given out. (The Old Pony Route is named only on Harvey's maps, but appears also on the OS Outdoor Leisure. It contours White Side at 700m and drops over Brown Crag to Thirlspot.)

Glyn dived into a residential side-street to change into his flat shoes. He'd been running a bit too fast for me, so I trotted on, enjoying a rest until he caught up. However, the road becomes dual carriageway. Maybe Glyn would take the other branch and overtake me in the dark. So maybe I'd better run the dual carriageway, just in case, and the dual carriageway joined back up again in the dark without my seeing it, so that was even more running. By such tricks does Nature ensure that we finish the trip at respectable speed.

But a human sort of speed trick lay before us. On a brow ahead, a parked car shone full beam into our eyes, and two fluorescent jackets stepped out. "We thought you were some kind of crazy people," says

A wintry scene on Nethermost Pike with St Sunday Crag behind Photo: Jon Sparks

Glyn tactlessly, "shining at us like that." Ah no, the crazy people don't have the word POLICE stencilled onto their cars. And it is, of course, us who are the suspicious characters. Glyn has been seen changing his shoes in the side-street, and there have been burglaries.

It takes the police a mere moment to decide that we're not burglars. How come? We are dressed as burglars, in long-sleeved jumpers, black tights, and sinister woolly hats; we carry dim lights. But perhaps the perceptive officers have observed the Wythburn mud that coats our thighs. Anyway, they say they can tell we're not as suspicious as we look, but would we mind explaining what we're up to?

When questioned by a Police Officer, frankness comes before modesty. We tell them about Skiddaw, and Scafell, and the Pike, and Helvellyn.

"Well, I can see you're enjoying yourselves, so we'll let you get on with it." I look at Glyn in the light of the police car. Glyn looks at me. It hadn't been altogether obvious at this point in the run, but now the perceptive and polite officer points it out – yes, we are enjoying ourselves. "Thank you for stopping for us," the policemen say.

"If we hadn't, I'm sure you would have chased us down and arrested us."

"Ah – but would we have been able to catch you?" They were, as I said, very polite police officers.

The usual effect of a police trap was reversed. After our brush with the law, we started going faster than before. It wouldn't do for them to come back past us and see us walking. And about a mile before we expected it to, Keswick appeared at the bottom of the road. The town closed in over our heads. People in pub doorways looked at us, shook their heads, and looked again. We ran in under the Christmas lights of the town centre.

It was half-past ten. We'd taken seventeen hours – not really a running time at all. But, despite the unpromising weather forecast, we had managed to make an interesting trip out of the Winter Threes.

Somewhere in the world there's a well-known (but probably non-existent) tribe whose counting system runs: one... two... three... a-heap-or-pile. Life there must be easy for accountants, and also for hillrunners; the heap-or-pile of Lake District Hills is not too troublesome to run over in a day.

Those of us educated within the National Curriculum, though, should be able to tell the difference between four and – say – forty-two. Forty-two hills make the Bob Graham Round, and the Bob Graham is a day's running that it's hard to beat. (It is, on the other hand, a day's running that won't find it at all hard to beat you. Less than half of those who start the Bob Graham finish it within the twenty-four hours.)

The Bob Graham, though, is not all that brilliant as a backpack route. It takes the long ridges and the popular stony paths, before plunging 2000ft into a valley for an insipid glucose drink and then back up onto another long ridge. That's not bad; but it's even better to explore not just the top edges but also some of the corners. There are hidden valley heads in the heart of these busy hills. There are slopes of rock and green grass where you're more likely to see a stonecrop than a coke can. There are mountains like Grasmoor and Swirl How to cross while the Bob Graham's ticking off minor summits along the Dodds ridge.

My idea was to do all this in two days, with a cosy bivvy at Foxes Tarn. It was an idea that a little hill-running dog of the Jack Russell breed shared entirely. However, the dog's owner didn't altogether go along with it. In the end the two-day run turned into a walk, and took me all year.

MAY: When you take a walker for a walk, you do have to be careful not to walk too far because they get unhappy. Hillrunners however intend to get unhappy. We don't even start to have fun until the rain's right down inside and trickling out of the trouser-bottoms; the food's all gone (or more conveniently, left behind right from the start to save weight); a couple of ankles have twisted, and it's getting dark. Ian, in particular, needs grief. Ian is preparing for a run of 450 miles, Land's End to Birmingham in ten days. He has to remedy the effects of months of road running in Warwickshire. I am to supply a weekend of intensive hill training, with added discomfort in the form of that bivvy on Scafell.

Scales Tarn makes a promising start. There's a certain amount of wind – enough to make the tarn splash away merrily somewhere in the mist, but not enough to pick the tarn up and fling it in our faces. We make the little dog an excuse for not doing Sharp Edge – the truth is that as runners we enjoy misery and exhaustion, but leave vertigo and terror to the rock climbers. We follow the entire edge of Blencathra, with a fine wind roaring up alongside the rock-towers, and then trickle down a long grassy slope into Glenderaterra.

Even below the cloud, there's enough rainwater in the air to conceal Keswick. The hand of man is evident only in harmonious field walls, in the terrace of an old track, in the slate slabs that cross the beck. Lonscale Fell runs along the dividing line between civilisation and the Back o' Skiddaw. At the Back o' Skiddaw heather grows high and hills are surly and shapeless. I like the Back o' Skiddaw for the simple reason that it doesn't much like me.

Away from the Back o' Skiddaw, Lakeland is friendly; Lakeland is also small (a really good runner, like Joss Naylor, can cover every summit in a week). It's just as well, then, that Lakeland has so much weather, so that different days can turn each single hill into several. Today, for instance, Lonscale Fell is a simple fence-end in the mist, and Skiddaw is a howling desert of pebbles. Last time, Skiddaw was a quiet grey place at dawn, and on the summit was a solitary walker playing tunes on a pipe. Contrariwise, Skiddaw-in-Sun remains for me an unclimbed Cumbrian mountain.

The little dog is starting to suffer; is the little dog really up to it? A stupid question – of the three of us, the little dog is the real runner. Little dog cheers up immediately we drop off the windy ridge – meanwhile,

Derwentwater and Causey Pike

two large humans are not altogether happy with the tilted slag-heap that forms the Bassenthwaite side of Skiddaw. We cheer up slightly as we drop below the cloud and discover that the slag heap is hanging above a long green valley with a lake at the end. Most steep slopes of Lakeland look across a sharp glaciated valley at another steep slope on the other side, but the wall of Skiddaw looks over Keswick and Derwentwater, along the length of Borrowdale, and into various of the green corners yet to be explored.

The Grasmoor group is where there are so many of the green corners that there's scarcely room for the ridges between. As a consequence, those ridges are squeezed up and pleasingly narrow: steep-sided and enticing.

Ian doesn't want them. Ian's dog wants them, oh yes, but Ian's dog has to go with Ian on a rather less up-and-downish route by way of Cat Bells.

Grisedale Pike is 'Lakeland's Matterhorn', and on the side of Crag Hill is 'Wainwright's Tower Ridge'. Well, once you've conquered the Matterhorn you need not fear a mere 2000ft rock climb on the side of Ben Nevis, so I traverse around the top of another of the green hollows to look at the Towers. The towers are not much looked at.

Their grey rock is covered in lichen and other plant life, they have loose bits, there is no obvious path at all. The drops alongside are not two thousand feet to a midsummer snowpatch and a Gaelic-named corrie; but they are, nonetheless, very definite drops. Wainwright's Tower Ridge is rather pleasant.

Ard Crags is pleasant too: a narrow strip of green leads to a high end with a tiny cairn and a bird's-eye view of agriculture. Ard Crags is more than pleasant, Ard Crags is perfect. Why have I never been on Ard Crags?

The perfection of Ard Crags is formed in layers. Part of it is its position in the walk, coming after the long, wet, windy crossing of Saddleback and Skiddaw. Part of it is my being alone, and somewhat tired, with evening coming on. But the main part of it is the shape of the place. It's a true summit – unlike, say, Scafell Pike – with steep slopes both ways, and the final tussock standing proud against the sky. The slopes are convex, they curve out of sight. It's just you, and the little cairn, floating above the valley. It's paragliding without the artificial assistance of the paraglider.

And you don't even have to go down any of those plunging convex slopes. Turning towards Buttermere, it's gentle grass all the way to Newlands.

There are runners on the top of Robinson – Bob Graham Round runners. Bob Graham doesn't have time for Wainwright's Tower, or the floating summit of Ard Crags; for these runners, Robinson is the final hill. The runners do not look particularly happy, so I try to cheer them up: ninety minutes, that's fine, you'll do it. But once they've gone, their feet pattering down the slope into silence, I recall that it actually takes a hundred and ten minutes to get from Robinson to Keswick. (If you knew for sure you could do it, you wouldn't bother to start.)

It's a lovely run down Dale Head to Honister, provided you don't have horrid heavy boots on. Two who do have heavy boots on are backpackers, mightily encumbered, taking all weekend to cover just fifteen miles around Derwentwater. I look at their big tent, and decide it would be unkind to mention the comfy bunkhouse at Rosthwaite. We are at extremes; they suffer with luggage during the heat of the day, I suffer with lack of luggage during the cold night. But I do my suffering while asleep, so I have the better of it.

Ian, at Honister, has decided not to suffer at all. He's going to hitch down the road and recover his car.

What does the guide do when the guided one has decided to accept no more guiding? Inertia carries me up the tramway. Shall I continue around the Scafells and the Conistons, over ground I know rather well, in grey weather? Can I even reach the projected night-spot of Foxes Tarn? The second question answers itself. Campers at Honister are already questing around after that elusive patch of dry flat ground; the night is rising gradually out of Borrowdale to join the grey cloud above.

I consider the summit of Great Gable. There are places in the Lakes that I go out of my way to visit, plan devious start-points and end-points simply to compel myself into. Even though it is higher and harder to get to than the summit of Ard Crags, the summit of Gable is not one of those places. It is covered in bare trampled stones and cairns. It is flat.

It has three ways up it, and each of the three is even steeper, even stonier than the other two. A warm sunny day becomes a sweated labour on those slopes. After such work, a long pause to enjoy the view... the summit of Gable is wide and high, and has no view. The crags and green valleys are too far down to see. You can look at near-by piles of stones, and through the heat haze to the similar pile of stones that is Scafell Pike.

That's Gable on a nice day. At nightfall, in cloud, there can be few places as inhospitable as Great Gable. Any other mountain has patch-es of grass tucked into the corners of crags. Scafell, that I'm not going to get to now, has the green lawn around Foxes Tarn, with sheltering screes on three sides and a view out through the gap to Eskdale. Great Gable has stones.

Grey is as grey does, and Great Gable is starting to seem like an interesting proposition. I take my bivvy-bag up onto Great Gable.

The summit of Gable certainly is extremely stony, but none of the stones is big enough to provide shelter from the brisk drizzle. The best I find is a small patch of moss. I've slept on such moss before, but never for very long; it takes about half an hour to sink through to the stones below. I search, less hopefully now, for gravel. I bend ever clos-er to the ground as the light fades away, but there is no gravel.

There are one or two mountains that really aren't suitable for sleeping on: Sgurr nan Gillean on Skye, because you might roll off, or Everest, because of the altitude. It really seems that Great Gable may be another of them. I resign myself to the stumbling, sore-foot descent, in the dark, of one of those nasty ascent routes.

So where are they, the nasty paths? Their pale trampled stones don't show by torchlight, and as for cairns – in the dark everything's a cairn. I'm not going to find a nasty path, I might even end up in Little

Approaching Lingmell on the Corridor Route

Hell Gate.

But I don't. Looking for the path I find a flat place, and the flat place is covered in grass. The place is sheltered by a little outcrop, and the grass is deep and tufty. The tufts would shrug aside a tent; Gable summit is not a place for tents – what a silly idea. But between the tufts are hollows just right for a bivvy bag. The top of the Nape's Buttress makes interesting shapes against the mist – and then the mist parts, and there's a view. It's the good view, the view down between the rocks to the black hollow of Wasdale, with the gleam of the lake and the rising curve of Yewbarrow ('the other Matterhorn of Lakeland'). The view's only there for ten seconds, but ten seconds are enough.

During the night, it hardly rains at all.

JULY: A couple of months later I came back to the Four & More. I was supposed to be walking Wainwright, his Coast-to-coast from St Bees to Haweswater and Yorkshire. However, the Cumbria Coastal Plain soon persuaded me that it was far too hot to be anywhere except the tops – or else, perhaps, Eskdale with its green pools and high golden hillsides.

Mickledore, the highest pass in England, is a grim place when wind howls through the gap and rain runs down the rockface of Broad Stand. On a still, sunny July morning, it is almost equally grim. Heat buzzes off the screes of Scafell Pike; the grey volcanic dust of the screes rises into the eyes and seeps down into the socks. A raven croaks from among the black shadows of Scafell's North Face. Mickledore is a narrow edge of red earth and eroded scree, dropping two hundred feet each way before you meet a tuft of living grass. Ahead, the rock step of Broad Stand is frightening, while on either side the scree descents are merely unpleasant. The crags of Scafell provide a strip of shade, and water seeps off an overhang above and drops as crystal. It hits the path with a faint splatting sound, then sinks into the dust.

All this is very good in itself, even better when contrasted with the green hollow of Foxes Tarn that follows. A small, sensible family is occupying the lawn and paddling in the pool. They're in the right place already, and see no reason to visit the dry, untidy and unpleasantly hot spot that's the summit of Scafell Pike just half a mile away.

Sometimes, as on the elegant ridge of Grisedale Pike, it's fairly easy to ascend five hundred metres. At other times it isn't, and the broad featureless slope of Grey Friar, on an afternoon that's hot and getting hotter, is such a time. Without ever actually clouding over, the sky is gradually transforming itself from blue to yellowish-brown.

Once again I arrive on the high ridge at the time when everyone else leaves it. The air has thickened to a sort of soupy underwater. The Langdale Pikes are seen as through green ocean, and the Scafells, that I left only a few hours ago, aren't seen at all. The air is at blood temperature, and quite still, and almost I expect to see a slow shark come drifting through it, attracted by the feeble movements of my weakening limbs... The spars of a shipwrecked Halifax bomber project from Great Carrs.

Thunder grumbles: two thousand feet down the hill it's probably raining heavily. I swim on through the thickening air. Coleridge never voyaged in the Southern Ocean, so does Part II of the 'Ancient Mariner' derive from a Coniston hillwalk in hot July? Coming up to the summit of Wetherlam, I pass through a cloud of insects: the little black sort, all wings and legs, that are so hard to get out of your eye once you've blinked on them. But insects in the eyes won't keep me from my cairn, even if thoughts of lightening make me pass it by quite fast.

The triangle between Coniston, Chapel Stile and Grasmere is the low place of Lakeland. In any other hilly bit of Britain such low parts are chipboard plantations, or else they're bog. This triangle of low-level Lakeland has twelve tarns, three rivers and a lake at each corner. Bumpy oakwoods grow over the tailings of old slate quarries. After the hot hill, it's pleasantly cool below the oaks. The former roads of Lakeland, untarred and stony between high stone walls, lead round to a black waterfall.

The low-level triangle has its own low-level hill. Loughrigg has several dozen summits all covered in head-high bracken, and each little path does its best to run off in all directions at once. After the simplicities of

Swirl How and Scafell, Loughrigg is the hill to get lost on! Little paths run off through head-high bracken, and each little path does its best to run off in all directions at once. There are rock outcrops, and a small unexpected tarn, and I look across the lilypads and between two of the outcrops to the brooding shadow of Heron Pike. However, the little path has turned me through 180°, and what ought to be the brooding shadow of Heron Pike is actually the brooding shadow of Lingmoor...

Compass-bearings and a low pass lead on to the Rydal slope, where ancient bushes of juniper grow out of small crags. Darkness lurks under the leaves of the wood, but through the darkness gleams the white gravel of a new-laid path, wheelchair wide. Between the black tree trunks, the lake of Rydal lies under the purplish sky. It lies flat and quiet, but waiting to hiss and go pockmarked. It won't have to wait long. The air is heavy with raindrops ready to fall.

And fall they do: at first a splashing sound on the upper leaves, but the splashing moves gradually down through the dark canopy and soon hits the path (and me, of course). It releases the trapped smells of the past dry fortnight – leaf mould and garlic, but with a dark underburden that suggests this may not be the wood to bivvy down in. The wet streets of Rydal shine orange under the lamps, with the Wordsworth Bus Shelter offering a welcome haven.

In a damp dawn I went up Fairfield by its gentle south ridge, and down over Cofa Pike. But Yorkshire beckoned, and I turned off to cross St Sunday.

SEPTEMBER: The next part of the walk came almost by accident. Days were shortening, and when damp leaves are falling into Ullswater, I like to be around to make sure they're doing it properly.

I started my walk round Ullswater from Shap, just so's not to be obvious. Obviousness, though, took me by the nose and led me over Helvellyn, and down Swirral Edge to a bivvy on Sheffield Pike. Obvious isn't necessarily wrong. Sheffield Pike has grassy bedrooms for a hundred, each with private balcony looking all the way along the lake.

NOVEMBER surprised us, coming in along the A66. A lorry load of windows got scared on a small slope at Scales, and I sat behind it for an hour while it refused to go down. Snow-flurries rolled down the slope of Souther Fell, and then the gritter came. I went and bought Keswick's cheapest ice-axe, the CAMP jolly (£34.95 at Needle Sport).

Time behind the timid truck meant no time for Swirral Edge, but the Keppel Cove path is another nice way down to Greenside: it's a white ledge, with snow falling upwards out of the deep grey hollow on the right. Going back up the juniper zig-zags, I met a couple coming down.

"So how did you like Stybarrow?" I asked them. I'd followed their footprints, passed above them as they dropped into the Sticks Pass, then come round the bottom by a longer route. But when they said "Amazing! How did you know?" I was planning to murmur "elementary my dear Watson's Dodd", and point to the distinctive fescue grasses caught in the velcro of their gaiters. But there was to be no omniscience for me today. Maybe I know where they've just been on; but they haven't the foggiest...

The top of the Dodds is wide yellow grass, with bits of cloud to look at. The side of the Dodds, though, has a high miners' path around the head of Glencoyne. Steep slopes drop to a glimpse of Ullswater, and the narrow path scrambles over a rock and dips into the bottom of a waterfall. CAMP jolly hasn't really been needed along the top, but here in the valley I'm glad to poke its little spike into the frozen tussocks dusted with slippery powder. Would I be able to perform the ice-axe self stop on a thousand feet of frozen grass?

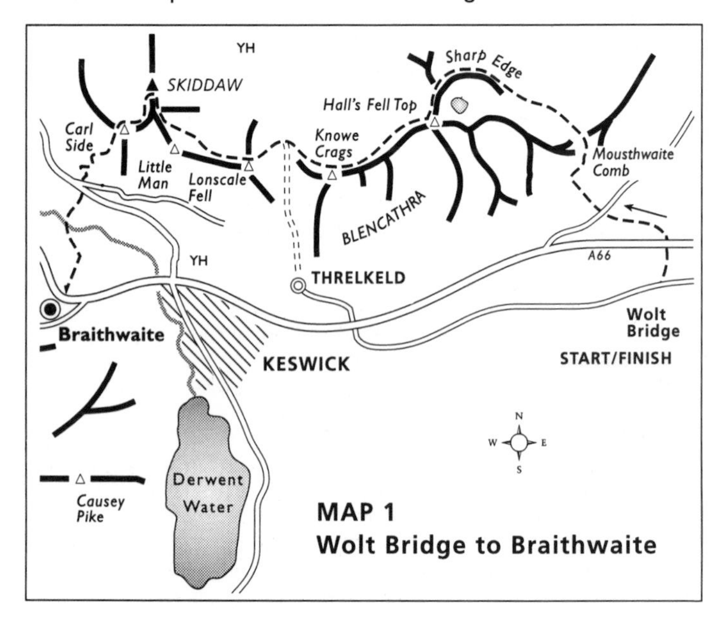

MAP 1
Wolt Bridge to Braithwaite

The little path from Brown Hills is picked out with white powder and shows well. If the white powder conceals black ice, this only helps me downhill quicker. The path out of Dowthwaite Head leaps up the hill-side in a single bound, a green ramp among bent hawthorns. Its encouragement is needed: the day is fading, and house-lights are starting to show along the bottom of Blencathra. And there's two miles of snowy tussocks to do before tea-time.

There's no time for sophisticated navigation, and anyway sophisticated navigation doesn't help along an invisible bridleway. I count paces from the plantation, take a bearing, and head out into the bog. The tussocks are iron-hard, and it's getting darker; but then I find, under my feet, a little stone culvert that must be the exact line of the invisible bridleway. So who's an unsophisticated navigator? I reach the track top with at least five minutes of usable daylight still in hand.

There's a footpath somewhere down in the fields, but why spoil a clever bit of navigating by getting lost? The frozen grass of the track centre crunches nicely. A necklace of linked headlights runs around the base of Blencathra. The orange streetlights of Keswick bounce down off the cloud, and in the east a few stars shine down on the snow-covered road. There's a phone box in Threlkeld, so I can ring Ian and tell him we finally finished our run.

Four and More: the Route

For those not staying at Scales' White Horse Inn, **Wolt Bridge** on the old road at GR358267 is a convenient pull-off for the car. (The car park under Mousthwaite Comb is very small, and should therefore be left free for daywalkers on Blencathra.)

From the bridge a tarred track leads northwards, and crosses the main A66 to become the access track for Lowside farm. Go round to right of the buildings, following waymarks, and slant up a field to the lane above. This leads left, to the small car park, and just past this is the start of the clear path up Mousthwaite Comb.

From the col at the head of the coomb, turn left onto a gently-ascending path that contours along the wall of the Glenderamackin valley. After a mile it turns up alongside the splashy Scales Beck, to arrive at the crag-circled Scales Tarn.

The ridge to right of the tarn is **Sharp Edge,** a Grade I scramble of considerable seriousness and exposure. An easier path slants up to left of the tarn to gain the skyline ridge, and continues with steep

Looking across to Blencathra

drops on its left to the summit of Blencathra.

SHARP EDGE: the path leading right from the tarn's foot soon gains the crest of the ridge; this crest becomes a rocky one. The rock is clean and firm, but there's a big drop on both sides. The gritty path down right is easier than the crest, though the crest is not hard and is probably safer than the path with its unstable surface.

The ridge butts against the rocks of the main mountain. The way continues inside a rocky groove on well used holds. Alternative routes offer themselves on the face to the left. At the top of the groove continue straight up, on rock, rather than heading left onto what appears as easier ground but is in fact a loose gritty surface. The summit plateau is reached quite suddenly, at a cairn. A short drop southwards and gentle ascent lead to the main summit.

Blencathra's small summit cairn is recognisable as it crowns the steep rocky ridge of Halls Fell, which comes up from the left.

Continue alongside the rocky drops and over one minor summit to the end of the plateau at Knowe Crags. Descend westwards, on steepening grass slopes, into the deep trough of the Glenderaterra Beck. Turn right on a broad path that runs above the beck, then crosses it on a footbridge. The path turns right, up the main valley, as the smaller path of the Cumbria Way joins from the left. Here continue ahead, uphill, into a boggy little corrie.

Grassy slopes between rocks lead up its head, where a fence guides left up the steep grassy slopes of Lonscale Fell. At the top of the slope is a cross-fence. Lonscale Fell's summit is through a gate and 50yds left, while the main journey continues alongside the right-hand fence to the gate on the broad Skiddaw path.

Cross the path onto the lesser one for Little Man, or turn up the main path to reach Skiddaw without its sub-summit. The final ridge of **Skiddaw** is stony with various cairns; the trig point at the far end is the top.

From the trig, return for 100yds only, dropping into the first small col and then climbing to a shelter cairn. Now slant down right, to find small cairns on a path leading down the west flank. This slants down into the col of Carlside Tarn.

Cross Carl Side, and descend its south ridge on a stony and fairly steep path to a quartzite outcrop called White Stones at the 500m contour.

A small path slants down the right-hand flank, to reach a wall below. It runs alongside and above the wall, to a stile that leads into forest at GR 251273. Turn left on the forest road.

The road descends gently round the hill, with splendid views, to a junction (GR 243269). According to the OL map, the path below, designated as 'Allerdale Ramble', starts from this point and slants. Unfortunately, it doesn't. Turn sharply left onto the lower road, and follow it east for 300yds. Now the small path descends, directly down a steep slope, through a gap in a spruce thicket.

After the first steep descent, the path bends left, then descends in zig-zags, becoming gradually clearer and wider, and emerging as a forest road at Dancing Gate (GR 244264). Turn right to reach the A591; then left, towards Keswick. There is a grass verge for the 200yds to a waymarked track on the right. This leads down to a bridge over the River Derwent. A waymarked path turns left, alongside the river, before farm sheds.

After a half mile (800m) the path divides at a stile and signpost. Turn right, not crossing the stile, with fence on your left. The waymarked path heads south-west, passing to left of Bog House to a footbridge, where it turns left alongside the ditch. It heads back right across a field with a single tree in the middle, to reach **Braithwaite**.

The little B5292 leaves Braithwaite alongside the stream, then bends away right and starts to climb towards the Whinlatter Pass.

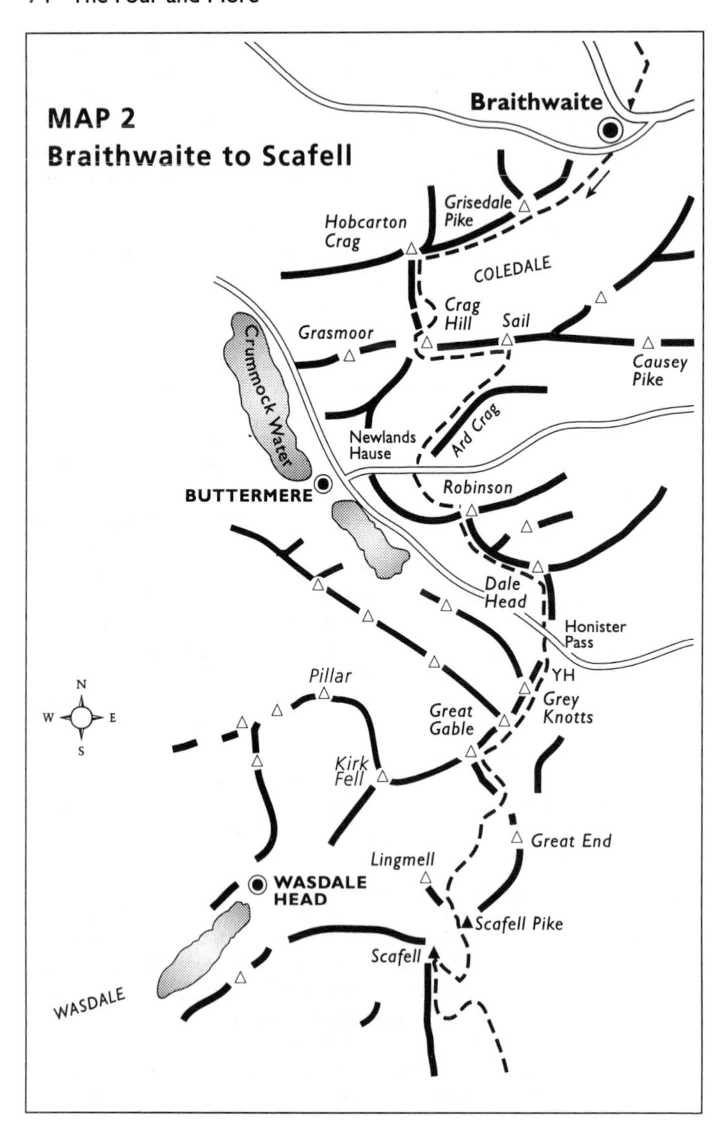
MAP 2
Braithwaite to Scafell
Braithwaite
Grisedale Pike
Hobcarton Crag
COLEDALE
Crag Hill
Sail
Grasmoor
Causey Pike
Crummock Water
Ard Crag
Newlands Hause
BUTTERMERE
Robinson
Dale Head
Honister Pass
YH
Pillar
Grey Knotts
Great Gable
Kirk Fell
N
W
E
S
Great End
Lingmell
WASDALE HEAD
Scafell Pike
Scafell
WASDALE

Pass through a small car park on the left, to where wooden steps start the hill path. This leads up the long, obvious ridge to Grisedale Pike.

The ridge and path lead down into the next col. Continue in the same direction, still descending, on a path that slants around the side of Sand Hill. This passes a fenced-off mine shaft on its way to the lower col of Coledale Hause.

The rocky ridge ahead can be taken up Crag Hill, but more interesting is the diversion to 'Wainwright's Tower Ridge'. Traverse left out of the col on very small paths across a stony and fairly steep slope. The towers on the ridge, which are quite small ones, are soon apparent on the skyline above. The ridge is clearly defined, with grass slopes beyond it on the left and steep drops on the right. Go up the crest, keeping close beside these steep drops. While there is no real difficulty, the rocks are seldom climbed, and you can't assume that absolutely everything is firmly attached to the mountain.

Pass round left to the summit of Crag Hill. A path leads down the rocky edge of Sail, and down to the col before Causey Pike. Here double back, to slant down the right-hand side of the ridge on a small path through heather. Cross the low, broad col, to go straight up the steep grass slope opposite. When the top is finally reached, the summit of Ard Crag is a short walk away to the left.

Return, and continue along the ridge crest on a small path. This gives a long, gentle descent to the double car park at **Newlands Hause**.

From the car park, two paths lead forward to the waterfalls of Moss Force. These are worth visiting, but a metal sign warns not to scramble up beside them onto the fellside, so that it is necessary to return to the car park for the steeper path on the right. Once on the plateau above, the obvious way is straight ahead to the base of Robinson, but the path follows the edge round to High Snockrigg; the path knows what it's doing as the direct route is swampy. The path to Robinson's summit becomes unclear as the slope steepens, but it doesn't matter as up will get you to the top.

From Robinson's cairn, a broad path leads south for 200yds to a fence, which guides along Littledale Edge. You could divert here to Hindscarth; but Hindscarth is much better ascended from Newlands, rather than by an acquisitive out-and-back from this path. The ridge leading onward to Dale Head is more enticing with its outbursts of rock. Dale Head itself has a fine columnar cairn.

From Dale Head's summit the path down to Honister heads south, to pick up a descending fence. Be careful here in mist, as the path is initially unclear, and a descent slightly too far west is liable to be rapid but unpleasant. The fence, once found, leads straight down to the mine buildings and youth hostel in **Honister Pass**.

Go straight across the road to a footpath sign 'Grey Knotts'. The slope ahead is steep, but a newly-built pitched path makes the climb easy. The path ends at a stile 200yds short of Grey Knotts' summit. But where is that summit, among the knolls and tiny pools?

When you've had enough of looking for it, head south-west along the remains of an iron fence to the cairn on Brandreth. The fence remnant continues to the tarns at Gillercomb Head, and now a wide path with cairns leads up onto Green Gable.

Eroded zig-zags lead down into Windy Gap. The path up Great Gable is steep and rocky, then crosses stony ground to the summit outcrop. This has no cairn, but there is the metal plaque of the Fell & Rock Club's war memorial.

The descent path starts eastward, and as it drops off the summit plateau becomes clear to follow, with large sprawling cairns. The steep part of the descent to Sty Head has been extensively rebuilt as pitched path: this was once the widest and deepest path in England, and said to be visible from Outer Space.

Go straight across the pass. After the stretcher box, cross a boggy area on large stepping-stones and then drop right for a few steps towards Wasdale. A path contours left, then slants to the right up the side of Scafell Pike: this path is the Corridor Route. It is well used, crossing bare rock as it climbs out of Skew Gill, and descending slightly on bare rock to gain the next stream gully. Ahead, the black jagged shape of Lingmell draws closer: the good way up Scafell Pike will be via the col to Lingmell's left.

The Corridor Path turns uphill, left, as pitched path within a scree. After 20yds, leave the uphill path at its first bend for a small path traversing out right. This crosses above the head of the deep gully of Piers Gill, then heads up to the Lingmell col. A wide path ascends left from the col to the summit of **Scafell Pike**.

Leave the summit by the way you came, but after 50yds bend round left, following cairns, towards the crags of Scafell. The path leads down into the sharp pass of Mickledore.

The ascent of Broad Stand is a short but overhanging rock climb with a drop below, and the scene of accidents: those confident in their rock skills can go down left for 20yds to the crack of Fat Man's Agony and follow the scratch-marks. The rest of us continue down the scree towards Eskdale, with the overhanging rocks of Scafell on our right.

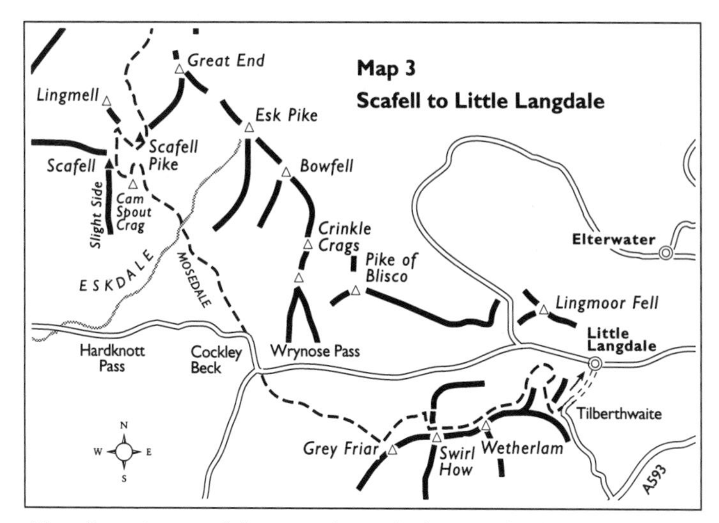

After five minutes of descent, the rocks become broken, and a small path leads right, onto the steep face. This path slants upwards, then runs level below the crags; it is easy to find in this direction, but narrow and quite exposed. It scrambles down a short groove to reach the top of a boulder gully. Turn up right for two or three minutes to reach Foxes Tarn.

From the tarn a pitched path zig-zags up the scree to the summit plateau. The summit of **Scafell** is 200yds to the left. It is very much quieter than that of Scafell Pike, and from it you look straight out of the Lake District, across Wastwater to the Irish Sea.

It's good to head southwards off Scafell. Just half a mile from the most popular spot in Lakeland, you're heading down a grassy ridge with no people, hardly a path, and nothing in front but the North Sea. The ridge is a nice one; the grassy spur off Long Green is a nice one (also a green, and fairly long, one). The only nastiness is what could happen of you go wrong – to right is a long, steep boulderslope; to left is a similar slope, with small crags added; ahead is a simply enormous precipice. In mist, therefore, it will be safer, if less exciting, to take the simpler route by Foxes Tarn (see *below*).

Descent from Scafell by Long Green: Go straight past Scafell's cairn and down the ridge of grass, stones and rock to Long Green (GR 210056), where the ridge turns right. Here drop left on a spur just south of east. The spur is grassy with some rock and a very small path. Descend it to a rock-knoll at the 700m contour (GR 214055).

This is the point where you turn left towards the How Beck. (This descent-line is 300yds to the right of the path marked on the Outdoor Leisure map.) It is important to identify the rock-knoll correctly. A hundred feet (25m) below is another rock-knoll, which is crossed by a stone wall. This knoll-with-wall is at the top of Cam Spout Crag, and it is the wrong knoll. If you reach it you must turn back uphill for two or three minutes.

From the top of the correct knoll, descend on a bearing of 60°: a cairn shows a possible line through the first little ten-foot crag. The descent slope below is grassy, with small outcrops of gently-angled rock. Go down with the big drops of Cam Spout Crag on the right, to meet the How Beck. On the other side of the stream is a path, which goes down beside it into Eskdale. The final descent to the valley floor is on bare rock beside the Cam Spout waterfalls.

Descent from Scafell by Foxes Tarn: (A safer route in mist): Return to Foxes Tarn, and descend the boulder gully already mentioned, to gain the narrow green valley running down from Mickledore. A small path leads down towards Eskdale: it does not follow the main stream, but one on the right that emerges from the boulder gully. It reaches the valley floor on bare rock beside the Cam Spout waterfalls.

Cross the River Esk and follow it downstream. It passes the mighty boulders of Sampson's Stones under Cam Spout Crag, and then runs below the small crag of Scar Lathing. Here the river turns right, towards the top of its gorge, but a small path runs ahead (east), though this will soon be lost. Keep the eastward direction, crossing lumpy grassland with small crags to descend to the Lingcove Beck. Cross the beck to the path beyond and follow it upstream.

Soon the beck turns left (north). Here turn up right to the grassy col at the head of Mosedale (GR 237040). Head down this valley, keeping to its right-hand slope rather than its boggy floor. An old track gradually becomes apparent, and leads to road near **Cockley Beck Bridge**.

Cross the bridge and turn right towards Broughton, passing a lonely phone box. After a few yards, go over the stile on the left and across a field to a step-stile leading over a wall.

The field above is pathless. Head round its right-hand side to a gate with stile at its top right corner. A green tractor-track zig-zags up beside the beck. Having lifted you almost to the 400m contour, it heads away east and horizontal, passing below the knoll called

Copthwaite How (GR 255013). Head straight uphill, on rough grass. A fence above has a gate and a stile at GR 257008.

This slope of Grey Friar seems endless. However, the grass becomes shorter, the ground rockier, and the view ever wider. Quite suddenly the cairn of Grey Friar comes welcomingly into sight.

A broad ridge leads across to Great Carrs. Near the top of the slope is a cairn commemorating the crew of a Halifax bomber of 1944. Follow the high cliff edge round to Swirl How, and go down its Prison Band, a fairly rocky ridge with views southwards along the interesting east face of the Coniston range.

After a direct initial ascent, the path up Wetherlam wanders left onto the northern face, traversing across the top of high slopes above Greenburn. Thus it avoids the small climb to Black Sails, while giving long steep views down to Greenburn Tarn.

From the summit of Wetherlam descend north-east along the fairly rocky Wetherlam Edge. Where the ridge levels off, a small path traverses off right to avoid the slight rise of Birk Fell, and then zig-zags down the head of Dry Cove to a miners' path. Dry Cove may be so called because it no longer contains a tarn; by any ordinary measure it's not particularly dry, but the track is good. It leads round left, onto a steep wooded slope overlooking the gorges of Tilberthwaite Gill, then slants down above the Tilberthwaite Beck to join a quarry track. Turn down past the cottages of **Tilberthwaite** to the small road.

Turn left up the road to High Tilberthwaite farm. A bridleway sign points into the farmyard, indicating the right-hand track beyond. It goes through a gate into a wood growing on quarry spoil heaps. This is an original Lakeland road, gravelled and stony between high walls. Ignore a lesser track into the wood, which is blocked by a gate. At a junction with a signpost, turn left for Little Langdale.

At the end of the wood, with the River Brathay visible ahead, turn back sharply right at a junction signposted 'Colwith, Skelwith'. The track dips to cross a beck, and becomes tarred. Pass through Stang End, and at the following farm, High Park, bear left into the farmyard at a bridleway sign. Signs point the way through the yard to the broad path beyond.

Just inside the wood, the path forks. Take the left one, where a metal sign indicates the permissive path to Colwith. The river appears flat and unexcited: certainly not as if it's about to plunge over a fairly famous waterfall. But it is. Colwith Force is down in a hole in the wood, a double plunge into a black leafy pool. The path reaches the minor road (Little Langdale to Skelwith Bridge) just beside Colwith

Skelwith Bridge

Bridge.

Turn right, away from the bridge, for a few yards to a stile on the left signposted for Skelwith Bridge. The path runs up the steep riverbank, and then turns north-east, to cross the driveway in front of Low Park. It turns half-right, east, towards the buildings of Park Farm, and passes to right of them onto their access track.

Turn left, through the farmyard, onto a small track that leads to Park House. Go down its driveway for 100yds, until it bends right towards the road. Now keep ahead on a path through a field and into a wood, with the main road nearby on the right. The path reaches the first house of **Skelwith Bridge** and joins the road. Turn left over the bridge.

Cross to a minor road with a 25% hill-climb ahead. Turn right at a tee-junction, and right again as a slightly less minor road is met. After 20yds a tarred track on the left leads towards Tarn Foot farm (camping). Turn right before the farm, following bridleway waymarks. After 50yds, do not bear left ('Grasmere, Loughrigg Tarn') but go ahead through a gate onto a stony track between walls.

The track climbs, then turns right into a wood at a slate sign 'Ambleside'. Climb through the wood on earth and tree-roots to a gate. The path now runs east above a wall and below the bracken of Loughrigg Fell. Ignore branch-paths on the left and follow the wall

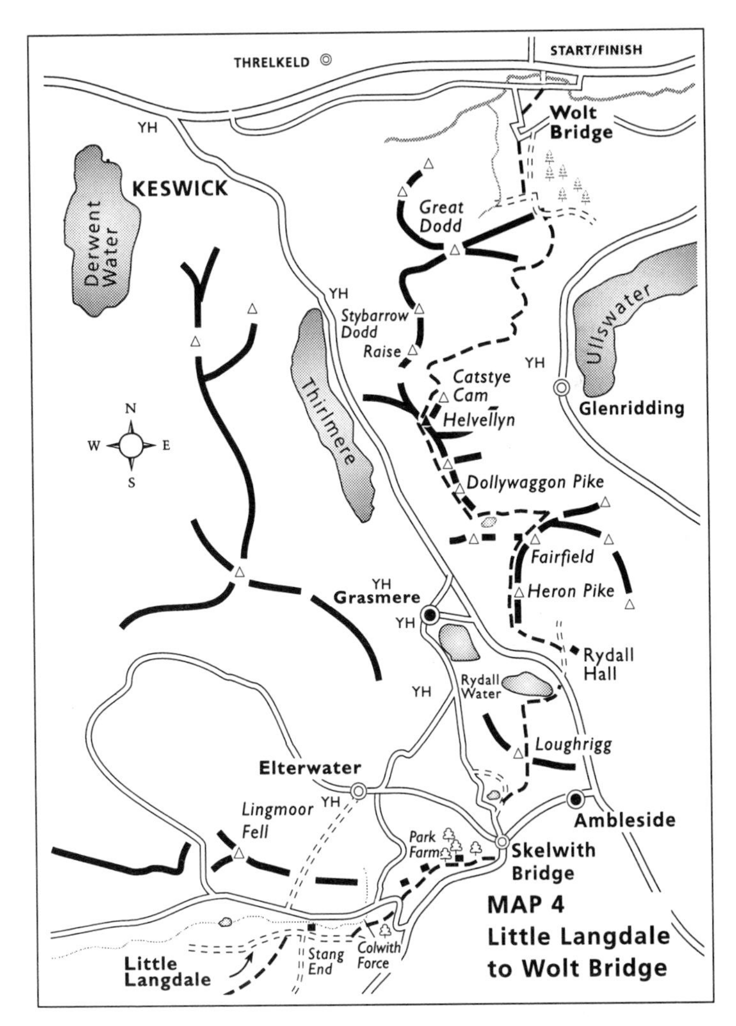

MAP 4
Little Langdale to Wolt Bridge

round below Ivy Crag. This high wall conceals a view of Windermere.

The path bends north-east and climbs beside a stream, then turns right to cross it. From here our desired direction is due north, towards the cone of Heron Pike, but with the bracken at its summer height, we want to get north on paths. So stay on the wide path, eastwards as it is, for 50yds, and then turn sharp left on a small path back to the stream. Just before rejoining the stream, an even smaller path heads slightly east of north. Follow this for 200yds. It is joined from the right by a slightly larger path, and this one runs, as desired, due north.

It crosses a low col between hummocks, and descends a cragged valley with juniper trees. At the foot of the slope it runs into a wood, and joins a wide gravel track. Follow this to the right, through the woods, just above **Rydal Water**. If you're lucky enough to be doing this bit between midnight and 6am, you'll enjoy it as Wordsworth did. At other times of day, you'll realise why he was so dubious about the proposed carriage road to Ambleside. Traffic noise carries well across the still waters of the lake, and swirls along with the morning mist around the islands.

The track becomes a small lane with houses. A gate on the left lets you down through a wood into a field. Go down the right-hand edge to a footbridge into **Rydal**.

Take the road uphill on the left opposite Rydal Lodge, to pass Rydal Mount (Wordsworth's place). The road ends at a farm. Go to right of a building and bear left onto a recently rebuilt path. This climbs a steep bracken slope, with views back to Ambleside. Above the crags of Nab Scar, the path finds a gentler ridge, with rocky knobs, grass, and a little stream down to the right (useful water).

The path leads on over Heron Pike, and above the deep empty hollow of the Rydal Beck, to Great Rigg. This is the gentlest of ridge walking. Even the final climb to **Fairfield** is not particularly steep.

Fairfield's summit area is confusing in mist; there are many cairns, but no paths as all is flat gravel. Head off northwards. A ridge soon forms, and becomes a steep spur. This descent is being eroded to bare rock, and when that process is finished it will give an entertaining scramble, but meanwhile it's awkward with loose scree lying over. A col leads to the perfect small peak of Cofa Pike, with its rock gendarme and its narrow arete. But the place lasts no longer than its name, a pleasure that's over in less time even than an Ambleside ice cream.

The ridge levels – this col is Deepdale Hause. At the far end of the flat stretch, at the very foot of the rising ridge to St Sunday Crag, a small path leads down a scree on the left. After a hundred feet (30m) of descent, the path traverses back left under some rocks, and makes its way slantingly down the steep face to the foot of **Grisedale Tarn**.

Cross the outflow, and take the eroded path up the flank of Dollywaggon Pike. The descent from Fairfield has been delightful, but now we must pay, with a thousand feet (300m) to climb up a path as nasty, steep and stony as any in the Eastern Lakes. At last it turns left and traverses, passing a decorative metal gate post. It leads to Helvellyn, but it's better to go up to the right and take smaller paths along the tops of the east-facing cliffs. Thus you cross Dollywaggon and Nethermost Pikes: thus you look into deep corries with their crags and tiny tarns, and all along Ullswater to the distant Pennines.

The obvious way northwards is the long, wide ridge to Clough Head. But the un-obvious way is better here. That way starts with Swirral Edge, and continues along narrow paths halfway up the eastern flank.

After **Helvellyn's** stone-built trig point, continue along the edge for 100yds to the top of Swirral Edge. An eroded path leads down very steeply to the beginning of the rocky ridge, just below.

This, the lesser of Helvellyn's two scramble-ridges, is a popular descent-route for those who've come up the Striding one. The descent is rocky but not difficult. At the foot of the rocks, ignore the path that leads down right towards Red Tarn; our way continues ahead up the grassy ridge to the conical peak of Catstye Cam.

Traces of path lead off down the western face, but these are soon

Swirral Edge and Catstye Cam

lost, and it's a steep, rough descent to Brown Cove. Cross the stream – notices warn not to do this by way of the concrete dam, which is crumbling from the bottom upwards, leaving a flying buttress of rotten concrete. A path beyond leads downstream, becoming a wide green track as it approaches the buildings at the head of Glenridding.

As it passes above a footbridge of the Glenridding Beck, the track divides. Take the left, uphill, branch, which becomes a terraced track that zig-zags above mine tailings and through a wood of junipers. At level ground above, cross an iron-and-concrete footbridge, and continue ahead to the foot of the huge hole of the disused Greenside Quarries. Cross the gravel arete that is the lower rim of the hole and traverse out right on a small path.

This passes above the col of Nick Head, and becomes a narrow and interesting path around the steep head of Glencoyne. After any reasonable rainfall, many waterfall streams splash across the path as it circles the valley's head and traverses out along its northern side. As the slopes above become less steep, a small path, with a cairn, heads uphill – but if this path is missed, keep going along the traverse path to the broken wall, and strike uphill alongside that.

Cross the boggy spur of the Brown Hills and descend northwards, crossing the Little Aira Beck, then slanting away from it. The ground is wet, but a useful small path can be found. Head for the nearest, southern, corner of the fenced enclosures. A kissing-gate marks the top of the path down to **Dowthwaitehead** (rather east of where the map marks the right of way).

The car park at Glenridding is the biggest and busiest of them all. Less than three miles from it is this quiet green hole in the hills. Stone walls criss-cross its floor and surround the stone farmhouse. Nobody comes here, despite the fact that it's a very much nicer place than the car park at Glenridding.

Turn down the tarred lane to the end of the buildings. A gate above, signed in slate 'Groovebeck', leads to the bottom of a slanting green path. This path, zooming up out of the valley like a jet plane taking off, was visible as you dropped towards the farm. It leads into the little col between High Brow and Low How. All good things must come to end, and this path ends here, leaving you to make your own way down the reedy beck to the Coach Road.

Turn left along the track, crossing the ford and footbridge of the Groove Beck. The track bends left and passes the top end of a plantation. A quarter-mile (400m) after leaving the plantation, a bridleway turns off right across the moor. The turnoff point is opposite a little dry gully in the slope above the track, but the bridleway is not signposted or visible on the ground.

The small stream alongside the bridleway line moves downhill very slowly in its bed of rushes, and so will you. The next two miles are not nice. There are tussocks, and the ground is wet, and the edge of the moor gets no closer. Aim for Souter Fell, or use a compass bearing. If the compass bearing is very accurate, you may come across a tiny stone-slab bridge where the bridleway crosses a side-stream. The fence at the NT boundary has a stile – this is at a fence junction GR 360237. After the fence the going becomes less horrible. Pass to right of the farm sheds at Lobbs onto a gravel track.

Now a footpath runs ahead, but it's simpler to use the track, turning left along the minor road at the bottom. At Wallthwaite farm is a signed and waymarked footpath on the right. It leads between the farm buildings and across three fields to Wolt Bridge.

DISTANCES

	miles	km	ascent	facilities
Start: A6 nr Scales				White House Inn
Braithwaite	12	20	1400m	Accommodation
Newlands Hause	19	32	1100m	
Honister	24	38	600m	youth hostel
Cockley Beck	34	54	1500m	phone
Skelwith Bridge	42	67	900m	hotel, cafe
Rydal	45	71	200m	hotel, B&B
Greenside			1400m	youth hostel, bunkhouse
A6 near Scales	62	98	400m	White House Inn
TOTAL ASCENT			8300m	25000ft

Accommodation is plentiful: the bivvybag can be unrolled on any of 27 summits (Cofa Pike alone being unsuitable). Accommodation with a roof on is less common. However, YHA members may notice hostels close to the route at Skiddaw House, Coniston Coppermines and Elterwater to add to the two on the route at Honister and Greenside. These remoter hostels are closed on one or two days of each week.

Pubs will sell you crisps and sweeties, but more wholesome food is hard to find – there is no shop at Skelwith Bridge, Braithwaite, Loughrigg Tarn camp site, or Rydal. A short diversion can be made to Coniston, Elterwater, Ambleside or Glenridding.

Cooking in a bivvy bag is not enjoyable. What is enjoyable is a slow civilised bar supper, followed by a late evening wander to the summit bedroom of your choice. In this context, the twelve-inch Cumberland sausage at Skelwith Bridge is of particular relevance.

OLD COUNTY TOPS

The circular walk from Grasmere over Helvellyn (Westmorland), Scafell Pikes (Cumberland and England), and Coniston Old Man (Lancashire)

Distance: 35 miles, 56km: height gain 10,000ft (3600m)

Many of us would like a long walk in Lakeland, but nevertheless think 45 miles is just plain silly. The circuit of the Old County Tops has many advantages. It is absurdly long, but not quite so absurdly long as the Threethousands. It has virtually no road walking. It has Grisedale Tarn at dawn. It has Eskdale, and those who love Lakeland love Eskdale the best. And finally, when the Threethousands Walk is doing a slow up-and-down to touch the trig on Helvellyn, this one is on a long ridge walk from Coniston Old Man, watching the sun sink into the North Sea and trying to spot the Isle of Man. Over the top of Swirl How is not just the scenic, but also the quick way back to Grasmere – honest!

A village is a place with no cashcard machine, so Grasmere is still a village. Though now equipped with kissing-gates and waymarks, Grasmere's paths are identifiable as those walked by Wordsworth, and between the car parks the houses are still slate. Helm Crag reflects in the lake at sunset, and the ash trees drop their leaves onto stony roads just as they did under the watchful eye of Wordsworth's sister Dorothy in 1802.

The walk starts from the Stock Lane car park (GR339073) at the south end of the village. A footpath starts at the primary school, 50yds west of the car park. It runs north through fields near the Rothay to the A591 (Dunmail Raise) road. Walk north along the roadside footpath, past the Swan hotel, to the track end of Winterseeds farm.

Go up this track. At the farm, it bends left; here leave it through gates above. A rough tractor track leads up right, to bend left after a

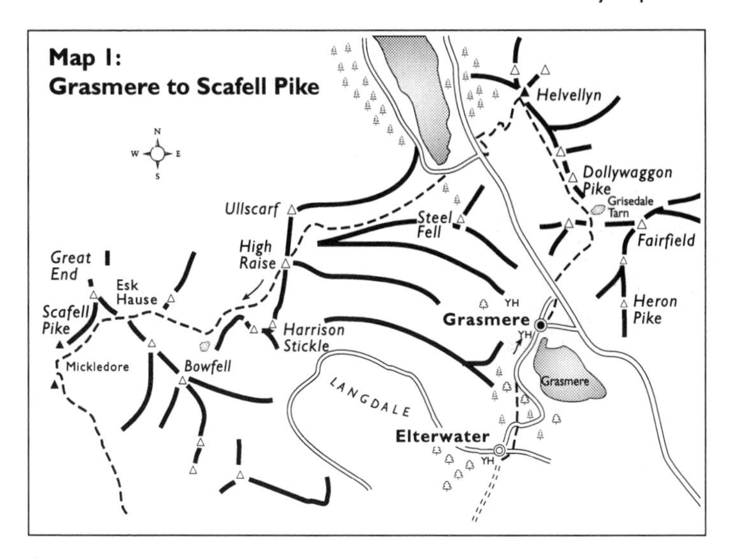

few yards. Here waymarks point uphill – there is no clear path, but at the top of the field is a gate with kissing-gate alongside.

Turn left with wall below and, soon, a wall above as well. A small track leads through a sheep-handling enclosure roughly paved with boulders. The well-built Tongue Gill path is now just below (this is the eastern of the two main paths to Grisedale Hause, marked as footpath rather than bridleway). Contour forward to join it as it rises.

This ascent of Helvellyn is pleasingly piecewise: steep sections are interspersed with flat, with the intended summit not even seen until the final ridge. The wide, well-sheltered path leads gently up to waterfalls, and then more steeply into a high combe littered with fallen boulders and frowned down upon by crags. If there is such a thing as a comfortable way of gaining a thousand feet this pitched path is it.

Grisedale Hause is a pass of the traditional type, a high notch in the skyline. Grisedale Tarn, lying below slopes of grass, is less spectacular than any of its approaches. However, it makes a cosy campsite, and on any Summer morning bright tents cluster at its outflow.

A small path turns left at Grisedale Hause and traverses to the col above the head of Raise Beck. A couple of streams on the flank of Seat Sandal are the last water before the Wyth Burn. Circling above the head of the tarn, you won't disturb the campers enjoying their lie-in on

Striding Edge, seen from the summit of Helvellyn, but not walked upon

soft grass below. You'll also get views across the water to the misted hollows of Patterdale, with a bright glimpse of Ullswater.

Go straight up Dollywaggon Pike on grassy slopes alongside a broken wall to meet the big path that crosses the top of the slope. This broad high way now traverses to Helvellyn on the western flank, trying to enjoy a view of not-very-beautiful Thirlmere. It's little extra effort to go straight up, and follow the eastern precipices over Dollywaggon and Nethermost Pikes. The going is grassy, the views are splendid, with Striding Edge not the only interesting eastern ridge. (No Striding Edge for us today. Never mind, Helvellyn's not a hill to do just the once.) The broad path is rejoined for a moment at the col north of Nethermost. Leave it at once to find a narrow one traversing the eastern brink.

Helvellyn's summit is a busy place, and even if you reach it at breakfast-time you may find people up from the day before – it's Britain's most slept-on summit. (I don't like strangers in my bed, so I prefer to sleep on Sheffield Pike.) The old border of Westmorland and Cumberland strides grandly along the Helvellyn ridge, and the summit is in both counties.

Helvellyn

Turning back down its western flank, though, we definitely enter

Cumberland. We enter Cumberland, perhaps, in some perplexity – the summit area is so trampled that it's hard to find the path, even though it's the very same path that we came up on. In mist, start from the stone shelter-walls to find the first cairn. This is the one commemorating the two airmen from Gosforth, and from it the path is clear. It wanders back into that col north of Nethermost. Now it takes the lower (right-hand) fork, slanting gently down across the slope. Having circled the head of the Comb Gill it turns back right and drops steeply into the hollow. It zigzags above the top of the trees, then goes down through them, crossing a forest road, to Wythburn Church and car park.

Take the track to the left, above the church. Just above the main road, a permissive path runs left under the trees for half a mile, to a road junction. Cross onto the minor road opposite, which is signposted 'Armboth'. Follow it for a quarter of a mile, to turn left up the track past West Head farm. Note that this farm is named as Steel End on the map (with West Head being shown to the north). The bridleway sign 'Dunmail Raise' is plain enough, pointing up past the buildings to a second sign pointing right 'Footpath Wyth Burn'. A track leads along the bottom of a wood. Cross two ladder stiles to the stream side.

Wythburn Church is a popular and sensible starting-point for Helvellyn, but as a start-point for Scafell Pikes it was downright perverse. So the path up this stream side is a small one, and not many people enjoy the traverse up the valley with the birches and babbling stream below and the waterfalls at the exit ahead. (Those coming down the way on the walk of the four Threethousands are too busy dreading Helvellyn to appreciate their surroundings.)

At the top you arrive suddenly in a wide bog-bowl. The stream becomes peaty, with water-lilies. Craggy lumps surround it: some are named peaks, and some are mere distractions. It's a fine place to get lost in, and often used for that purpose by walkers on Wainwright's Coast-to-coast.

The path continues up the left-hand side of the valley, keeping to the foot of the slopes on the left to avoid the former tarn bed (now swamp), then climbs gently into the upper bog-bowl. Here ignore the map's right-of-way line, which is unhelpful. Keep left along the bottom of the firm ground, to meet a clearer path joining from the left at GR 294103. (This path has come up out of Far Easedale.) The new path leads easily up right, to the pass of Greenup Edge immediately north of High Raise, though you can also strike straight up the rough grass

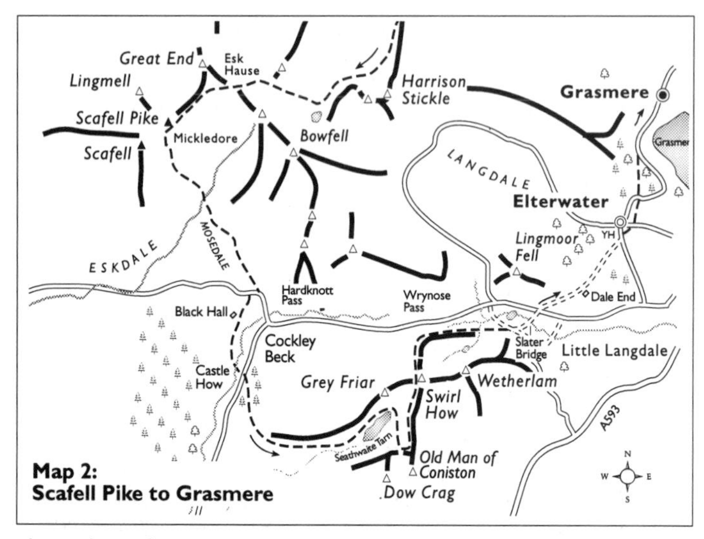

Map 2:
Scafell Pike to Grasmere

above the path.

High Raise is an undistinguished hill of high flat grass. It's not clear where they found the stones for the masonry trig point. Its purpose on this walk is purely as an obstacle: to go round it would be even more tiresome.

Slant down grass slopes south-west, pass through moraine hummocks to north of the Stake Pass, and join the path running west out of that pass. This traverses below the ridge of Rossett Pike to Angle Tarn. It has enticing views into Langstrath, the second most deserted dale of Lakeland. You could abandon Scafell Pike aspirations and descend into Langstrath, certainly. But we are about to go to Upper Eskdale, which is the one dale that's even more deserted than Langstrath...

And the Scafell Pikes are now not far. At Angle Tarn we join their large and popular path from Langdale. Mind you, it's still possible to get lost at Esk Hause as a selection of large and popular paths cross this complicated col. At the stone shelter-structure bear left, still uphill, to reach a crossing path at the upper col after five minutes. Turn right on this cross-path, which rises gently around the flank of Great End. This highway is not the most interesting way up Scafell Pikes, indeed it is the least interesting. Still, it's pleasant to mix with the colourful horde, interact a bit with the fellow-humans, maybe let slip that you've arrived by way of Helvellyn.

The path crosses the boulderfield of Ill Crag, and dips; crosses the boulderfield of Broad Crag; and dips: and climbs steeply to Scafell Pikes.

Scafell Pikes

Scafell Pikes, so fervently desired by so many, is not a wonderful mountain. A wilderness of stone, mostly rearranged by the hand of man and sprinkled with orange peel, the best thing about it is the view of its wonderful neighbour Scafell. Persons of true taste and discrimination may prefer the eighteenth-century version of this walk, whereby Scafell is the high point of Cumberland and the Pikes a mere outlier. (Note that Scafell Pikes lost its final s at about the time Cumbria lost its three separate counties.)

The path for Mickledore leaves Scafell Pikes, confusingly, in the direction of Lingmell for its first 50yds, before bending left towards Scafell. Scafell Pikes may not be a wonderful mountain but Mickledore, the gap between it and Scafell, is a wonderful pass, a knife-edge leading to an overhang. Turn left to go down below the crags of Scafell. After an initial scree, the Foxes Tarn path comes down in its boulder-gully from the right. Now the descent is grassy, beside a chuckling stream. Such lightheartedness: this is Upper Eskdale, this is a serious place. But the beck doesn't seem to be aware of the grim crags frowning down onto it, and flings itself in gay abandon over a couple of high waterfalls. The path scrambles down bare rock on the left. And now we're in Upper Eskdale.

The valley floor is grass and bog, with a river winding over gravel. The valley walls are a selection of crags, and above them the Scafells, and Esk Pike, and Bowfell, and the Crinkles. Now, the essence of Lakeland is pay-and-display machines, and pitched paths, and people with dangling map-cases. In Eskdale are none of these, for Eskdale is a place apart. Either Eskdale isn't proper Lakeland – and indeed, Eskdale has no lake – or else only Eskdale is and the rest of Lakeland isn't. On a Summer afternoon, Eskdale is a deep bowl of damp sunlight. Even the occasional Eskdale rock climber climbs in silence, and can be identified as a small coloured splodge, like some rare lichen, among the acres of grey. Eskdale's rock routes, classics of fifty years ago, are too far from the car for today's climbers – and, perhaps, too easy.

Cross that boggy valley floor, and the gravel-bottomed river, to a path that goes downstream on the left bank. On the hottest afternoon,

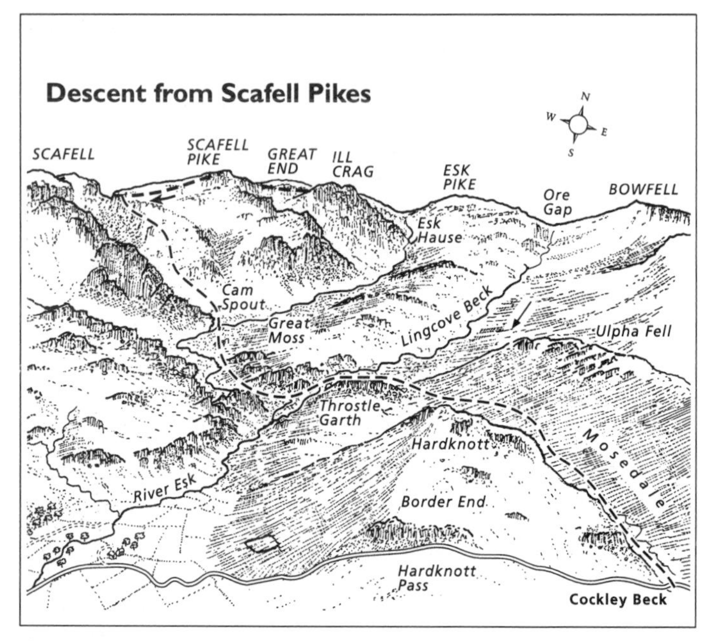

the green pools of the Esk gorge are ice-colour, and they're also not far off ice-temperature: a more effective refreshment than the ice-cream and beer that this valley so sadly lacks.

The river bends right to drop into the gorge, and here keep ahead (east), following a path that soon disappears. Cross the Lingcove Beck, and the path above, to the low col at the head of Mosedale. Once you've found this col among the knolls and confusing contours, the flat boggy valley beyond is the quick exit from Eskdale. After a mile of bog-trotting, a stony track is found to right of the stream. This leads quickly down to the tarred road at Cockley Beck.

To the right, the road rises in zig-zags to Hardknott, with family cars in low gear going up and down like beads on a string, or like children on a helter-skelter. None of them actually requires to get from Eskdale Green to Little Langdale, any more than walkers need to travel from Helvellyn to Coniston by way of Scafell Pikes.

Turn right, to the bridge at the foot of the road's steep climb. A signed (but untrodden) bridleway leads down left, through Black Hall.

Here the bridleway ahead (not the footpath to the left or right) leads to the bank of the Duddon.

Follow the river, past the first set of stepping-stones and the rock-knoll of Castle How, to a second set of stepping-stones with ford alongside (GR 239001). Leap lightly, from stone to stone, into Lancashire. Turn right along the road for 200yds, then turn off right, before an Outdoor Centre, on a field footpath. After 200yds, regain the road by turning left to a ladder stile, going straight across the lane onto a path under the pines of Pike How Close. The path rises to join a broken wall, then drops sharply to cross a small stream. Go up through bracken, now with the wall to the left, to reach the top of the forest under White How (GR 240993).

The wall turns to the right (south) across the slope, and the small path traverses below it for 400yds to an empty gateway at a rock-knoll with a rowan tree. The knoll looks down on green Dunnerdale.

Duddon, despite its tarmacadam road, is scarcely busier than Upper Eskdale. To the west are only small hills, not mentioned in Wainwright. To the east is the Coniston Old Man massif – but this is its grassy backside, the side further from the motorway. So this valley doesn't bother much with walkers, and attends to its ancient business of keeping sheep. With its lush grass, its sheltering trees, its crisp stone walls, Dunnerdale is particularly good at keeping sheep.

Turn left through the empty gateway, and take not the steep path ahead, but a gentler one sloping up to the right, passing below small outcrops. This grassy side of Coniston is good in its way. Its way is a twisting one, that creeps up on the mountain, mooching round a grassy corner like some world-weary detective and finding, without surprise, the corpse of a tarn: the Seathwaite reservoir.

It's best not to hang around the scene of the crime, specially as that scene is a fairly dull one, a bog below slopes of grass and boulder. The path on the south (right-hand) side of the tarn is small, rocky and rather nice: the one on the left-hand side is flatter and faster, to a boggy crossing around the tarn's head. The slopes up to Goats Hause are gentle and grassy, and not at all like the steep stony routes from Coniston village. Sneak up on the mountain gradually, and let it surprise you, at Goats Hause, with a sudden view to Dow Crag.

Below your toes, scree drops for five hundred feet to Goatswater, a grey tarn in a desert of stone. Beyond, in the open country of the South, an end of Coniston Water glitters, and a yellow glow of sunlight is on the mud of Morecambe Bay. The day fades towards evening, and the rocky outline of Dow Crag (the mountain) stands black

On Scafell Pikes, looking across upper Eskdale to Bowfell

against the bluest part of the sky, with boulders and hillwalkers crisply silhouetted. Dow Crag (the crag) is lost in the shadow, though the voices of late rock climbers float across the air: "I'm coming up now, very slowly..." Turn left on stony path to the final county top.

Coniston Old Man

The Old Man's summit is a domed cairn, like a bowler hat perched on his bald head. Now you look down past the real tarns – Low Water, Levers Water – to civilisation. Civilisation is not distant, but it is a long way below. And looking down the sunbeams, past the crags and the ravaged mining area, the Civilised Lowlands are curiously flat and dull: far less worth looking at than Dow Crag reduced to abstraction by low backlighting, or Harter Fell's crinkly pyramid, or the sharp little shapes of Sellafield against the sea.

We turn north, now, and enjoy a classic hillwalk while most hill-walkers are down enjoying the pub. The path is wide and friendly, though the right-hand side of the ridge drops away suddenly to the copper mines. The Scafells look a long way away – as indeed they are – and Helvellyn is lost in the haze somewhere on the far side of Civilisation. The air is cooling, and the western sides of the rocks are

Looking from Swirl How over Brim Fell to Coniston Old Man (L) and Dow Crag (R)

going all golden.

After the gentle climb to Swirl How, follow the clifftop round left – west, then north – to Great Carrs. Ahead, the long ridge of Wet Side Edge descends in a gradual and grassy curve, just right for very tired walkers. Greenburn Tarn is down on the right, while down on the left is the car park lay-by at the Three Shires Stone.

Down there, our three Old Counties meet. The Lancashire/Cumberland border follows the Duddon to Morecambe Bay – the Lancashire/Westmorland one runs down the Brathay to Windermere. Only the Westmorland/Cumberland one takes the high line over the fells, crossing Bowfell, the Langdale Pikes and High Raise to the Dunmail Pass; then running along the Helvellyn range from Dollywaggon to Stybarrow before dropping into Ullswater.

As the sun sinks, the views of Bowfell get better and better. From the ridge-end knob, the path slants down the right flank. The first stone wall crosses ahead: turn right, in front of it, to cross the Greenburn Beck on a new footbridge.

If there was anyone else left on Swirl How, they thought Grasmere was rather a long way away, wasn't it? It would be – for those encumbered with cars. But for walkers it's a mere four miles from the bottom of the hill: four miles of lowland paths, and wildflowers, and woods. A track runs down beside the beck, becoming tarred as it passes the first houses, one of which is a climbers' hut (Low Hall

Garth). After another 200yds turn left on the signposted footpath to Slater Bridge. This has two high slabs to cross, and a narrow arch of drystone wedged slate. There can be no finer way to re-enter Westmorland.

Take the worn path ahead to High Birk Howe and the road beyond. Cross to follow a tarred lane opposite, marked 'Unsuitable for Motors'. Somehow the lowlands have changed now you're down in them – no longer flat and boring. No longer boring, as sunset repaints the fields and trees in the harsh metallic green you normally only see on sports cars, with the waters of Little Langdale Tarn supplying the shiny chrome trim. And – sadly – it's no longer entirely flat either. You've been climbing ever since Slater Bridge, and there will be a rather bigger climb (Red Bank) before you get to Grasmere.

But the slope that'll really make you suffer is the downhill one that comes next. The lane becomes a track that descends into Elterwater in big round pebbles, shut between high walls. The fact that it goes down through a lovely wood is neither here nor there. At last it reaches a road that runs down by the youth hostel into the village.

Having reached Elterwater, take the road on the right ('Ambleside'). Just outside the village this reaches the B5343 at a T-junction. Go straight across onto a bracken path to left of a stream, and up to the Red Bank road above.

Go up the road, then turn off left, uphill, on a path that passes an electricity transformer station. The path climbs steeply but briefly up a stream to cross a col (GR 336056) and descend northwards into Nicholas Wood, the last and loveliest of the woodlands.

Grasmere the lake lies below, with Grasmere the village tucked up under Helm Crag and half-asleep already. High above, the gap of Grisedale Hause doesn't look like something you scampered up into in sixty minutes, full of early-morning vigour.

The path drops through the wood, becoming a tarred lane and then joining the Red Bank road at Hunting Stile. The road winds quietly into Grasmere and stops.

It's been a trip through History, through three non-existent administrative areas and up a forgotten mountain called Scafell-Pikes-with-an-S-at-both-ends. But now it's time for the modern world, with its cars and camp sites. Wild Lakeland is all very well, but there is something curiously attractive in the evening tea-room, the cafe and the pub. If we want any more landscape we can buy it at the Heaton Cooper Studio in the morning.

Note: A time and distance chart of the walk is in the 'Guidance' section on page 156.

Roamin' with the Romans
Windermere to Penrith over High Street

The Lake District makes one last rocky stand at High Street before letting the Pennines take over. I've heard it said that there is nothing worth bothering with east of the Kirkstone Pass, but I'll have none of it!

It's true that the range is less intensely rocky than the Scafells or Helvellyn. Soft grass replaces stony paths, and a single weatherbeaten fence-post stands in place of the usual crowded cairn. But, if you're trying to do a twenty-five mile day, it does make sense to do it where the slopes are slightly less steep – where you can stride out without stubbing your toes against a boulder – where you don't have to keep stopping to empty the scree out of your socks.

That's what the Romans thought, anyway. And the Romans should know. After all, they were the long-distance walkers in days when not getting to Penrith by nightfall didn't just mean a nasty night out in an orange bag. It meant getting slaughtered – and eaten, as well, if bears got you before the Britons did.

This is not simply a walk from dawn until quite late in the day; it is also a walk from today back to the dawn of History. Before they were convenient railway stations, Penrith and Windermere were Roman forts of Brocavum and Galava. (The railway station's in the wrong place: Galava was actually at Ambleside.)

Between the forts, along the very top of High Street, ran the highest Roman Road in Britain. It was built between 80 and 90AD, along the existing line of an ancient Celtic track known as Brethestrete – the Britons' Road. The broad, flat ridge of High Street was more appealing to the Roman engineers than the scrub and bogs below. The

Above left: Thornthwaite Beacon; above right: The Cockpit stone circle on Moor Divock

bare mountain was free of wolves and bears, and any attacking natives would arrive at the roadside slightly out of breath.

For much of the way, the Roman Road is still being used as today's path. Today's walkers, though, must veer aside to touch the trig; and so, at various places on the north side of High Street, Roman stones lie undisturbed among the mosses and bog grass. Here it is easy to imagine damp legionaries marching through the mist, dreaming of olive groves back home.

Although flat on top for faster walking, the High Street area has its share of precipices and pointy peaks. At the southern end we give an energetic alternative over three tops that are actually sharper and more mountain-shaped than the rough lumps around Langdale and Borrowdale. And for the whole of the range the comfortable grassy ridges lie above glacier-carved corries, dark crags and sparkling tarns.

The route is fairly easy to follow, apart from the first three miles on the lower ground. There is only one steep section – even that isn't very steep – and most of the route follows gently undulating ridge. The smoothness of the ground means that in mist it will need careful use of the compass. The Romans are supposed to have sped along at five miles an hour. This would suggest a time from Ambleside to

Penrith of about five hours, but the Roman mile was a flexible measure: a thousand double paces of fully-loaded Roman soldier. Miles on the slopes were therefore shorter than those on the flat.

Start: Windermere railway station
Finish: Penrith Castle and railway station
23miles, 3700ft (36km, 1100m)
Maps: Landranger 90 (Penrith) and a mile of 97 (Kendal); or Outdoor Leisure Maps 5 and 7

The walk starts directly opposite Windermere railway station where a narrow road is signposted 'Footpath to Orrest Head'. The road winds steadily upwards for about half a mile before it becomes a stony track. On reaching a clearing the path splits into three. All paths lead to the top under tree cover, but the right hand one that follows the wall is the most direct, arriving at a T-junction. Turn right, passing a line of benches, to an iron kissing gate; now it is only a few hundred metres to the rocky outcrop of Orrest Head.

'Orrest' means battle, although baffled historians can find no record of any battle on Orrest Head. Scafell Pike and most of Southern Lakeland can be viewed from here, and the ten miles of Windermere basking in the Grizedale forest. Indeed, Baddeley's guide described this view as one of the finest and most extensive in Britain. Those of us who think the view from the top of High Street is even better are quite wrong. "High Street," says Baddeley, "is one of the least interesting of mountains." Any who believe Baddeley should turn back now, and take the train to Penrith!

Otherwise, leave Orrest Head in a northerly direction on an indistinct grassy track descending to a joining of walls. After crossing the wall continue the descent until you reach a minor road. Go right along the road for 150yds to locate the farm of Near Orrest. A public footpath to Far Orrest skirts to the left of the farmhouse to some stone steps embedded in the wall. Cross the next field diagonally to a wooden stile and follow the path to the farmhouse of Far Orrest. Yellow arrows show the way to the right of the farm through a couple of wooden kissing gates. Then go immediately right along a walled green lane until the path divides. Take the left track through a gap in the wall. A final pasture brings you out at the Ings-Troutbeck road.

Take this road right for 200yds to a bridleway lane marked 'Kentmere and Garburn'. After about 800yds it deteriorates to a

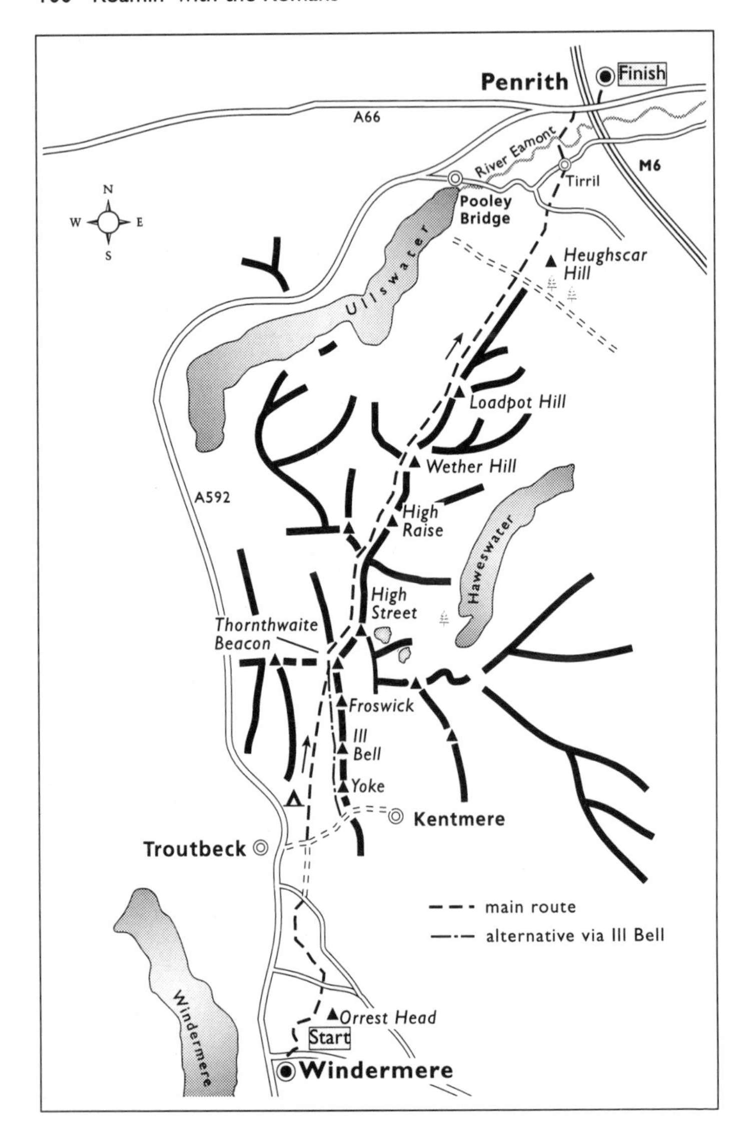

Penrith
Finish
A66
River Eamont
M6
Tirril
Pooley Bridge
N
W
E
S
Ullswater
Heughscar Hill
Loadpot Hill
Wether Hill
A592
High Raise
Haweswater
High Street
Thornthwaite Beacon
Froswick
Ill Bell
Yoke
Kentmere
Troutbeck
main route
alternative via Ill Bell
Windermere
Orrest Head
Start
Windermere

stony track that is followed into the Troutbeck valley. This passes below a plantation to a track junction at GR417027.

Here the High-level Variant, described at the end of the chapter, branches off to the right towards a second small plantation. The main route goes through the gate on the left, and takes the form of a pleasant terrace walk along the Troutbeck Vale. The narrow stony path passes above the campsite of Limefitt Park, to which there is an access track. Those departing Windermere late in the evening may wish to make use of this conveniently positioned site, which has a shop and even a pub.

To the west, beyond the campsite, the whitewashed cottages of Troutbeck village are strung out among the lush green fields below the crest of Wansfell Pike. The views to the east are restricted by the steep bracken-covered slopes of Applethwaite Common. The finest aspect is to the north where the long spur of the Tongue dissects the valley. Further to the right the shapely trio of Yoke, Ill Bell and Thornthwaite Crag command the attention.

The next mile and a half (2km) are straightforward as you pass through Long Green Farm to the old Park quarry. Troutbeck was once an important slate mining centre, output being at the highest in the late 1790s; now only the slag piles remain.

The only tricky bit on this section is keeping your feet dry when negotiating the ford (GR424050) at the foot of some pleasant cascades.

After passing the quarry the path descends to a wooden bridge crossing Hagg Gill. Climb up to a gate to meet the path from Troutbeck, then turn right continuing along the valley for three quarters of a mile (1km). The next part is where the steepest section begins as you ascend the path known as Scots Rake. As the name suggests, this track is the route the border raiders took for their forays into Troutbeck and was the scene of many a battle with the inhabitants of the village. The initial stages of the Rake are not obvious. Aim for the wall in front and follow it for about 200yds, then turn NNE on a green path.

It is difficult to imagine Roman chariots tackling these steep slopes and it is thought that they made more use of pack horses and slave-borne litters. The stiff climb of 450m (1500ft) will leave you breathless, but the retrospective views of Windermere provide a plausible excuse to break the journey. Near the top the route levels out and meets the track from Froswick.

At the top there are some iron posts that could prove a useful guide in mist. If time permits a short detour to Thornthwaite Crag is

High Street from the Straits of Riggindale

recommended, if only to admire the impressive cairn, which is an eerie sight when stumbled upon in the mist. Although it is an easy couple of miles to High Street there are some misleading paths in the direction of Mardale Ill Bell. The wide tracts of black peat speckled with white gravel rise gently before curling round the western side of High Street to reach a dilapidated wall after a mile (1.5km).

The main path continues alongside the wall to the summit, but the Roman Road continues on the western side of High Street parallel to the ridge, taking the form of a wide green track. Old stonework can be seen embedded in the peat. It is while on these bits that we can visualise the Roman soldier in his full glory. He had not yet refined the art of backpacking. Wearing a metal breastplate and carrying two swords, a javelin and cooking utensils with a combined weight of around a hundred pounds, he must have looked like a forerunner of an ironmongers' rep. There were no Gore-tex boots for the Romans; they wore hobnailed sandals. There can be little doubting the fitness of these warriors carrying such weight over long distances.

From the road the most prominent feature is the rock-splattered bank of Gray Crag, which sweeps into the wild coombe around

Hayeswater. To the left Thornthwaite Crag and Stony Cove Pike occupy much of the frame. The Fairfield group and Helvellyn with Striding and Swirral Edges are also impressive from here.

To locate the trig point you will have to strike up the higher ground to the right. The place to leave the road is marked by a small pile of rocks and is easily missed. A narrow sheep path leads directly to the top. A gap in the wall reveals the summit marker; there is also a small shelter.

High Street at 2718ft (828m) is the highest point on the walk, and the highlight of the day. There are superb views of both Lakeland and Pennines.

In the eighteenth century the fell was called Racecourse Hill, referring to the shepherds' festival that took place on the summit every 10th of July. The official reason for the meet – of returning stray sheep to their owners – was made the excuse not only for horse-racing but also for fox hunting, wrestling and the consumption of vast quantities of local ale, lugged in barrels to the ridge. A second festival in November coincided with 'tupping time', the mating season. The autumn festival took place in the Dun Bull Inn at Mardale, where the beer was more convenient.

To fully appreciate the eastern panorama it is necessary to walk out to the edge of the plateau. Blea Water is two hundred feet in depth – the deepest tarn in the Lakes. Its rounded outline is embraced by the sharp ridge of Rough Crag on the left and the expanse of Mardale Ill Bell on the right.

Although there is a clear path northwards off High Street just to right of the wall, to use it would be to miss some of the best-preserved sections of the Roman workmanship. Unless you need the wall to provide shelter from wind and rain, it would be better to return down the western side to rejoin the Roman Road. Descend moderately in a northerly direction for a mile (1.5km) to the Straits of Riggindale.

The wild recesses of Riggindale gained fame as the hiding place of the Kings of Mardale. Hugh Holmes was caught plotting against King John in the Canterbury Conspiracy of 1208. He was fleeing towards Scotland but stopped off here, married a local women and took refuge in a cave beneath Kidsty Pike.

At the far end of the valley Haweswater Reservoir can be seen beneath the tree-covered knoll of the Rigg. Whenever I gaze upon this tranquil lake I imagine what life would have been like in the village of Mardale before it was flooded in 1941. Manchester

Corporation acquired the land in the 1930s and the local farmers gathered for years in the Dun Bull knowing that their tiny community was under sentence of death by drowning. (A rather extreme case of watering down the beer.) In times of drought the outlines of the village can be traced on the exposed mud of the reservoir bed.

Go through the gap in the wall (GR 440122), bearing right and keeping close to the rim of the Riggindale valley. The main path continues ahead to the Knott: Kidsty Pike lies round to the right: both these paths are better defined than our one leading to High Raise, which can be confusing in poor visibility. Two hundred yards up from the low point of the col the path forks. The main path and wall continue ahead, but take the right branch, keeping close to the rim of Riggindale. Looking back from this path, the course of the Roman Road can be seen carving its zig-zags deep into the broad peat breast of the slope you've just descended.

As the path turns east and starts to descend towards Kidsty Pike, head north-east along a faint track that dips into a grassy col and begins the gentle ascent to High Raise.

The small pile of stones that marks the second highest point of the day is about 70yds to the right of the path. From the top the best views are of the valley of Martindale leading to Ullswater. The lake is divided into two sections by the rugged mass of Place Fell.

The ridge wall is now running on the right, off our route; but in mist it provides a useful guide, even though huge chunks of it are missing. Descend to a gate and fence, which is followed to the right and crossed by a stile. The path becomes soggy underfoot as we pass Redcrag Tarn. This algae-infested pool of brown water was a watering place for horses, but looks unsuitable for human consumption, and anyway you would probably be swallowed up by soggy peat long before getting to the water's edge. The path is sandwiched between fence posts and a drystone wall.

A further mile claims Wether Hill. Its second hump is crowned by a small cairn. The ridge dips slightly. Shortly after the path begins to rise again, passing Lowther House, now a pile of rubble but once a comfortable shooting lodge. The chimney marked on some older maps fell in the storms of 1973.

Loadpot Hill is the last peak on the ridge. From the grey stone trig point that hails the top, Blencathra and the northern fells loom large. Ahead the many paths traversing Heughscar Hill can be seen carving their way over the fell. Further north, wild yellow grasses yield to green chequered fields and the market town of Penrith at journey's

Wintry scene showing Blea Water and the head of Haweswater

end.

The Roman road now skirts the north-western flanks of the hill as it begins a gradual three-mile (5km) descent. A few paths will try and entice you left, but ignore these. The track reaches level ground at the stone circle known as the Cockpit (GR 483223), one of the many legacies of the Bronze Age.

After crossing Elder Beck the track starts to rise gently, to reach a stony track – the place is highlighted by a wooden signpost and an untidy cairn. If time is short, the easy track to the left will take you down to Pooley Bridge. Otherwise take the green track ahead, signed 'Roman Road Celleron', along the western side of Heughscar Hill.

Dark peat has given way to more subtle green grasses interspersed with smooth white limestone. Heughscar offers the best views of Ullswater so far. Ullswater is Celtic for bend or elbow, and aptly describes the dog-leg shape of the lake. Pooley Bridge lies on the old Westmorland/Cumberland boundary in the foreground.

The cart track passes above a plantation before reaching Winder Hall. A field path on the left then brings you to the road junction near Celleron. If the field path is missed the track leads to the road 200yds

Yoke, Ill Bell and Froswick

farther east.

The next section of the Roman Road is not a right of way, the line of it passing through cultivated land. Therefore we must follow the narrow, high-hedged lane ahead (or to the right, if you missed the field path!) for about one mile (1.5km). Turn right, into the village of Tirril.

Just before the Queens Head pub, a public footpath to Penrith is located on the left side of the road. Follow the beck into a small wood until it emerges at a lane. Cross the lane and continue through a couple of fields to the river.

A newly-constructed wooden footbridge is just ahead, and this leads to a field path to left of a wall. The path passes under the railway and reaches the A66 at the edge of Penrith.

High-level Route to High Street via Ill Bell

If the Romans had invented the roller coaster, the ridge path over the peaks of Yoke, Ill Bell and Froswick would surely have been the inspiration. This alternative is much better than the lower path, as its elevated position affords splendid views over the Troutbeck and Kentmere valleys. However the walk is slightly longer, has an extra 700ft (250m) of ascent, and is not strictly the course followed by the Roman Legions – probably because they didn't do this sort of thing for pleasure.

Instead of going through the gate above Limefitt caravan park, continue along the main rough cart track as it begins a moderate ascent to the Garburn Pass. The route passes some woods and joins another track from Dubbs reservoir. One hundred and fifty yards before the gate at the top of the pass, a track marked by a small cairn bears left towards Yoke.

The path cuts a corner to reach the wall and climbs grassy slopes to a ladder stile. The path, lighter in colour and much wider, ascends steeply on the Kentmere side of the mountain. The summit of Yoke is soon reached. From Yoke there is an egg-cellent view of Kentmere, the Nan Bield Pass and the Pennines. Ill Bell, the finest of the three, occupies the ground ahead.

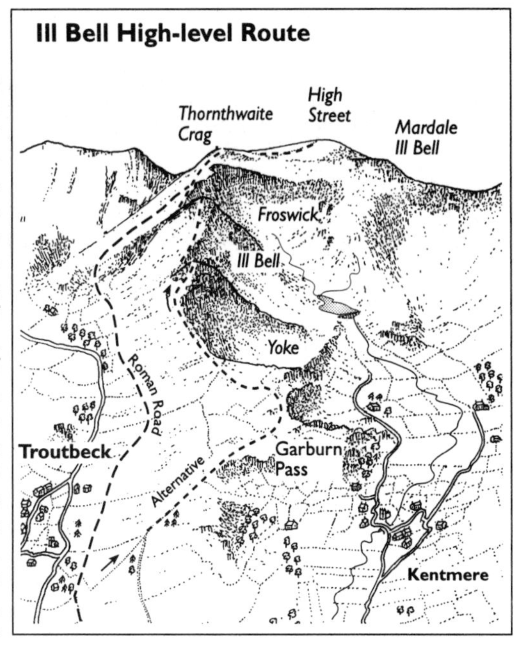

After a drop of 150ft (50m), the path rises steeply to the prominent summit cairn of Ill Bell. To the south, Yoke's Rainsborrow Crag can be seen at its best above the Kentmere reservoir. The full length of Windermere is visible with Morecambe Bay beyond.

Ill Bell is much rockier than Yoke and the exciting path weaves among rock slabs to the left of the second summit cairn. The descent of approximately 300ft (100m vertical) from Ill Bell is more acute than that from Yoke and is succeeded by a sharp rise along a green ridge to Froswick. Make the final descent from Froswick to the col where the main path to Thornthwaite Crag is met at the top of Scots Rake.

The Eight Great Horseshoes

There's something very satisfying about a horseshoe walk around one of the great Lakeland valleys. All morning you look across at the mountains you're going to do in the afternoon. At lunchtime you look down the length of the dale, over the top of the lake, and try to work out where the start point car park was. And all afternoon you look across with pride at the mountains you did in the morning.

You miss out, it's true, on the hidden valleys and interesting half-way-up-the-hill ground. To make things worse, even the greatest Lakeland horseshoe doesn't offer more than twenty-odd miles. Still, twenty miles is nothing to be ashamed of when they include seven thousand feet of uphill and maybe an exciting scramble.

So why not be for the day a top-contour woman or high mountain man? Each of these walks can be contrived to take in some unexpected territory; not one of them is entirely on the trodden pedestrian highway. And a slightly lazy day has its advantages. There's no need to crawl out of bed at dawn. At day's end, to console yourself for the loss of those summit sunset hours, you can take to drink in some convenient public house. Furthermore, if you adjust your walk clockwise, in step with the sun, you only need apply sunscreen to one side of your legs – a useful economy.

Great Hell Gate and Wasdale

On these short walks you'll have time in hand for getting lost, so you don't need route descriptions. We've put in a couple, anyway, to get you started. The other five we give in summary, with hints for avoiding the too-trodden paths by sneaking in a scramble round the side.

1: BUTTERMERE

S/F: Loweswater
Distance 19 miles (30km): Height gain 9700ft (2900m)

The fine ridges of the Grasmoor group are mostly transverse, so little use can be made of them on a horseshoe walk. However, we do get onto the fine ridge of High Stile and High Crag, and the fairly fine ridge of Robinson. Honister Pass offers a bus back to the start or a bed at the youth hostel, so that, of the big horseshoes, this may be the one to start off on. *Full route description follows on page 111.*

2: ENNERDALE

S/F: Ennerdale Water foot
Distance 20 miles (32km): Height gain 6800ft (2100m)
By way of Pillar High Level Path, Steeple, Ennerdale lakeside

A long circuit around a roadless valley, this is a fairly serious one. Gable being so often climbed it makes sense on this occasion to take the Moses Trod path that traverses attractively below the northern crags. The contour path north of Kirk Fell is also available, though if you don't already know it, Kirk Fell is worth a visit. Leave it by the rocky spur, marked with iron fence posts, that descends directly to Black Sail. For the High-level Path, Pillar Rock and Pillar see the Wasdale Horseshoe route description.

After Scoat Fell, the continuation by Haycock to Iron Crag and Crag Fell is grassy and pleasant – there's a descent path to west of Ben Gill. However, the descent over Steeple to Lingmell (435m) though shorter is even pleasanter. Finish along the south shore.

3: WASDALE

S/F Nether Wasdale
Distance 21 miles (34km): Height gain 9700ft (2900m)
By way of: England's fiercest, but particularly Scafell

Though the fiercest don't include Great Gable, as the traverse route below the Nape's Needle is a scramble Grade 1, and far better than the boulder-trudge over the top. This one is under-crag and through crag rather than ridge-walking, so it's a particularly tough one. However, there's always Wasdale Head to descend to, with the path along the foot of the Screes allowing retreat with honour to Nether Wasdale. *Full route description follows on page 117.*

4: ESKDALE

S/F Brotherilkeld
Distance 12 miles (19km): Height gain 5500ft (1700m)
By way of: Esk Gorge side, Scafell, Crinkle Crags

It's a shame to start with the Esk Gorge, as it makes such a fine finish. We do it to get the Bad Step on Long Top uphill, and also the route onto Scafell by Lord's Rake. A short but serious circuit: escapes to Langdale or Wasdale are long, and leave you hopelessly far from your car.

5: LANGDALE

S/F New Dungeon Ghyll
Distance 12 miles (19km): Height gain 5500ft (1700m)
By way of: Pike of Blisco Crinkle Crag, Bowfell Climbers' Traverse and Great Slab, Jack's Rake

Comparatively short, but full of possibilities. Rather than Pike of Blisco, ascent can be made by the easy but interesting Crinkle Gill (scramble Grade 1) or the rather harder Browney Gill (Grade 1). To reach the Great Slab of Bowfell, descend from Three Tarns down the Band for 200yds, then contour forward to join a small ascending path. This traverses right, across a very steep slope, to pass below Flat Crag to a spring. Turn left up a bouldery groove, to find the Great Slab on the left. This is very easy-angled and when dry can be walked up to Bowfell's summit plateau.

The descent of Jack's Rake (Grade 1) is for confident scramblers only. Dirt makes this one slippery when wet, and it is considerably more exposed than it feels. To find the top of the Rake, descend from Pavey Ark's summit SW over gentle rocks to a cairn and the end of a stone wall. Now go straight down SE on scratched rock to find the top of the Rake, a very clear groove slanting down left.

6: BORROWDALE

S/F Rosthwaite
Distance 15miles (24km): Height gain 6600ft (2000m)
By way of: Dale Head, Great End, Langstrath

Borrowdale Head is a junction of spreading side valleys, allowing a variety of horseshoes. Shorter ones include Glaramara; the longest starts over Catbells and ends by Watendlath. However, Langstrath is the finest finish.

7: CALDEW

S/F Mungrisedale
Distance 20miles (32km): Height gain 7500ft (2300m)
By way of: Bowscale Fell, Sharp Edge (Grade 1) Blencathra, Skiddaw

An austere exploration of unfrequented country. The hills are grassy, with a feeling of remoteness not found elsewhere (except upper Eskdale). To avoid the feeling that you could be in the Pennines, include the rocky Sharp Edge of Blencathra. Glenderaterra is deep but pleasing, Whitewater Dash shouldn't be taken in a hurry, and Carrock Fell has gabbro rock just like the Isle of Skye. Knott, however, is not exciting. *Full route description follows*

8: KIRKSTONE

S/F Glenridding
Distance 20miles (32km): Height gain 7600ft (2300m)
By way of: Striding Edge at dawn, Cofa Pike, Kirkstone Inn, High Street

Kirkstone Pass cuts the journey up – you may be tempted to cut it right in half and make it a two-day one. It would be nice to finish by way of Beda Fell or Fusedale, and use the Ullswater lake steamer to join up the two ends. However, the last sailing is at 6:20pm.

Around Buttermere – with Stile

In the Lakeland, where mountain is jammed against mountain to fill all available space, a high narrow ridge is fairly unusual. Here however is a route crammed with ridges. The outward leg treads the thin rocky edge between Ennerdale and Buttermere. Mist swirls up out of deep hollows on the north; the south is high steep screes. The ridge of the Derwent Fells is gentler, with long grass slopes dropping into Newlands.

The Grasmoor group has the finest ridges of all: pointed, steep sided and high. Unfortunately they are all running the wrong way and have to be crossed rather than walked along. Turn them upside down and you get the deep and steep Gasgale hollow which ends the walk.

The high horizontal ridges are traversed, alas, all too quickly. It is getting up to them that is the hard work and a walk that involves three distinct ranges is never going to be short or easy. However there are straightforward escape routes back to Buttermere at Scarth

Looking across to Buttermere and Grasmoor from Haystacks

Gap, Honister and Newlands that let you tailor the walk according to how well things are going. Honister Pass has a youth hostel and a bus service back to the start of the walk.

Start and Finish: Scale Hill car park, Crummock Water GR 149215
19 miles, 9700ft (30km, 2900m)
Map: Landranger 89 (West Cumbria) or Outdoor Leisure 4 (Lakes NW)

Head west along the road towards the village of Loweswater. After 200yds bear left at the 'Low Park' sign. Turn left across Park Bridge then straight away take the public footpath, marked 'Ennerdale and Crummock', on the right.

This path curves to the left and then goes along a walled lane to the right of a barn. The grass path rises steeply into Flass Wood, and turns sharp right to meet the wall at the top of the trees. Follow the wall to the point where it meets another wall descending the slopes of Mellbreak, and rake up the hillside on the left. This trail cuts a corner through the bilberry and heather to meet a wider path. Angle

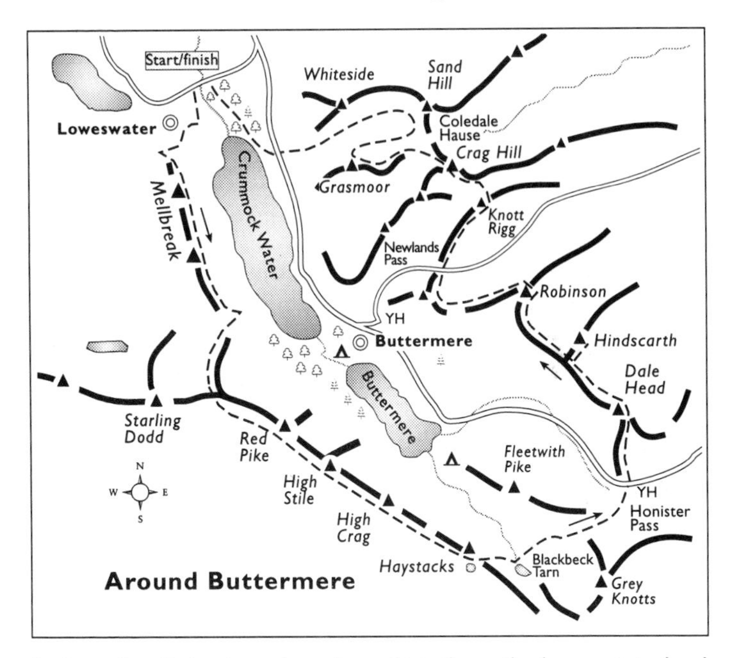

back at the diminutive cairn, after which the path changes into hard rock. The path weaves through the rocks encountering several ledges that offer exquisite views of Grasmoor End and the lake below. A narrow enclosed gully like a mini version of Lords Rake leads to easier ground. The last few yards are very easy going.

Head SSW for half a mile (800m) across the broad grassy plateau to find the second and slightly higher summit of Mellbreak. The plateau is difficult in mist and care should be taken to avoid the paths descending right into Mosedale.

After leaving Mellbreak keep to the right of some posts, descending Scale Knott to a gate. Go through the gate and, after climbing in and out of a beck, scramble upwards a few metres to the wide path that links Buttermere with Floutern Tarn. Scale Force, which lies ahead, is the biggest waterfall in the Lake District with a single leap of 120ft (38m) into a sunless, tree-filled ravine.

Ascend to the left of the falls on a steep well-worn path of red subsoil. As the stream enters the gentler upper valley, a narrower less defined path bears left up the open heather fellside to Lingcomb Edge. Now there's a final 250m assault on Red Pike, whose summit is crowned with a cairn and a crescent-shaped wind shelter.

There are brilliant views over the Ennerdale valley with its forestry conurbations and some eminent peaks providing the rearguard. Pillar, the Scafells and Great Gable are a majestic line-up with the distinctive Langdale Pikes peeking through a gap in the range. To the north-east the much photographed Bleaberry Tarn and the scarred path over the Saddle provide a dramatic foreground to the Grasmoor and Dale Head ranges yet to be tackled. Centrestage is reserved for the next peak of High Stile.

Leave Red Pike, initially south, then south-east along the edge above Chapel Crags. After a three-quarter mile of straightforward stony track and a modest climb of 350ft (100m) High Stile is reached. The best prospect is from the north-eastern promontory, where the mountain ends abruptly overlooking Buttermere village. Buttermere means 'lake by the dairy pastures' and from here we can see those pastures at their best.

One of the nicest bits of ridge in England is the all too brief section ahead between High Stile and High Crag. It has lots of secret niches overlooking magnificent Burtness Combe. The path now descends 300ft (90m) followed by a shallow climb of less than 100ft (30m) to gain the top of High Crag.

A new pitched path zig-zags down the eroded slope of Gamlin End. Though firm, the new path is extremely steep, and knee brakes will certainly have to be applied on the way to Scarth Gap Pass. There is a small rise over Sail before the pass is reached.

Haystacks may be lacking in height, but definitely not in stature. Numerous paths weave among rocky knolls and stumble on hidden pools of water. This is deceptively energy-sapping country. Take the new pitched path as it wanders to the left (the direct line will involve a bit of scrambling). The top itself is a twin peak with a narrow cleft between the two tops, and a small rock pool just in front.

An obvious path south of west makes its way to the left of Innominate Tarn. Wainwright made no secret of his love of Haystacks and, in accordance with his wishes, his ashes were scattered over this spot.

From the tarn continue in the same direction on a path that crosses the top of a cragged slope, overlooking the length of the Buttermere valley. After reaching Blackbeck Tarn, carry on up the short slope in front before passing just to right of Green Crag. Go immediately left of the rocky knoll of Little Round How and drop to the flat bog of Dubs Bottom.

After crossing the stream the path leads off left towards Buttermere. Ignore this and go straight ahead up the slope to the quarry workings. At a slate building turn right, following the old tramway to the embankment before descending the far side to the cluster of buildings at the Honister Pass.

HONISTER PASS

Cross the road by the youth hostel, and take the path going straight uphill to left of a wire fence. Ignore the one immediately left as this leads to some old mines. Having surrendered 1000ft (300m) since Haystacks we are faced with a tedious 1200ft (350m) slog over the wild grassy face of Dale Head. The beautifully crafted cairn overlooks the Newlands valley. Hemmed in by spectacular screes and red bracken coated slopes, the river snakes along the wild pass towards the bulk of Skiddaw.

The ridge from Dale Head is rather sharp at first, becoming a broad grassy promenade after a half mile. A metal post marks the side ridge leading off north towards Hindscarth – the peak baggers among you will simply have to have it.

The main ridge of Littledale Edge continues north-west, beginning the rise to Robinson. At the top of the steep grassy rise, the fence bears left and we leave it heading north for the last two hundred yards over stony ground to Robinson's Cairn.

Oh dear! We've run out of mountains again. Fortunately, there's a whole new range just across the road.

Leave Robinson by a small path descending to the splashy grasses of Buttermere Moss south of west. The first descent is steep, lasting a little over a kilometre. On the flatter ground stay on the left side, to pass near the tarns on High Snockrigg; for the best views of Buttermere and the best chances of surviving those horrid swamps.

Head north from the tarns (to avoid climbing the higher ridge of High Snockrigg) to a point on the plateau edge overlooking the Newlands Pass. A small path runs along the edge and down the spur left of Moss Beck to reach the car park on the Newlands road.

A path from the car park leads back right to let you view the impressive waterfalls of Moss Beck. There are notices warning of the dangers of scrambling around the top of the falls.

From the far side of the car park, a path climbs the spur of Knott Rigg with fine views of Addacomb Scar to the left. From the highest point of the ridge above Ard Crags, descend northwards to the depression at the foot of Sail, where you have to start regaining that lost 200m by the slanting path that heads first left, then right, to reach the col to the east of Sail.

A pleasingly sharp but short ridge is followed over Sail to Crag Hill, where a well-cairned track leads south-west for 400yds before going west to a grassy depression. Then begin the rise up Grasmoor's least interesting side to the flat top.

There are plenty of shelters from which to admire the panorama across Buttermere's deep valley to the morning's conquests of High Stile and Red Pike, which are severed by the torrents of Sour Milk Gill. On a clear day you can enjoy the Solway Firth and the distant Scottish hills.

There is a superb little path descending the ridiculously steep north-western side of Grasmoor immediately to the left of Dove Crags. But, at the end of such a long day, most will want a more reasonable gradient. Return to the wide dip between Grasmoor and Crag Hill and turn left at a wide path, which soon has a stream alongside. The path nears, but does not reach, the col at Coledale Hause on the right; instead turning left beside the stream and down into Gasgale Gill.

After the long valley walk the path heads across rough terrain to

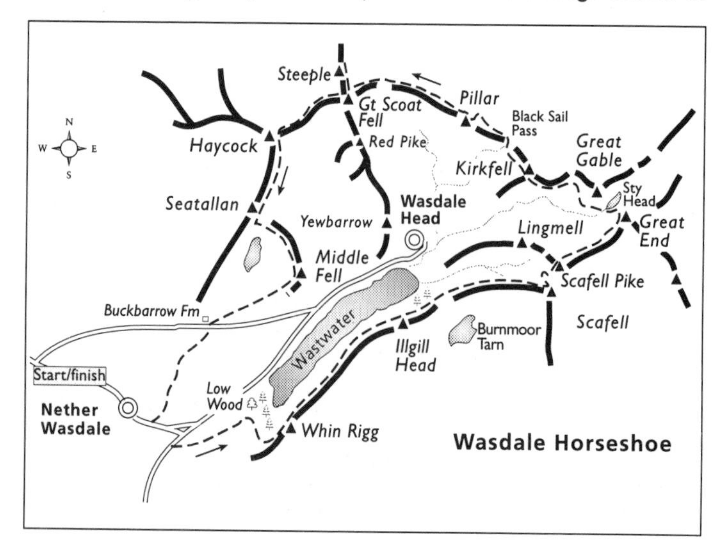

meet the road at Lanthwaite Green with its lonely telephone box. A footpath is indicated over stone steps to the right of the farm. Fences guide you round the farm though paths are a bit soggy. A footpath sign shows the way left into some woods via a kissing gate. A wide green road through the woods brings you back to the starting point and hopefully your car.

Wasdale Horseshoe Route

Wastdale, says Haskett Smith in his guidebook of 1894, is the Chamonix of England. When a man was in the Lake District for climbing, as opposed to Wordsworth-type daffodil-dreaming, Wastdale was where he went. And, despite its tarred road, despite its car park and camp site, despite losing a letter from its name, Wasdale is where that old adventure lingers.

For those sturdy Victorians in their tweeds and nailed boots, a day picking peaks around the perimeter was no sort of day at all. Gully-slime was there to get smeared with, precipices were for adding interesting uncertainty to an ascent, and the Nape's Needle was a place to fly your hanky as a flag from the topmost stone.

If you want peace and quiet, and soft grasses, go to the Back o' Skiddaw. If you want views, and ridges, and ridge-top paths, go to Buttermere. Ridge-walking, says Wainwright, is the best walking there is. But the intimate encounter with the crag goes slightly beyond what's normally considered as walking.

This walk has a great deal of uphill, and difficult and interesting ground. It'd be a shame, though, to hurry it. A bivvybag, unrolled at altitude somewhere between Scafell and Kirk Fell, may be the answer. If time does run out, the path along the base of the Screes is an appropriately rugged return.

Start/Finish: Nether Wasdale, small car park at church
21 miles, 9700ft (34km, 2900m)
Maps: Outdoor Leisure 6 and 4 (Lakes SW and Lakes NW)

Follow the road eastwards, turning right and crossing the River Irt. Just beyond the bridge a footpath sign points up the driveway to Easthwaite farm (do not take the bridleway just beyond). Pass to left of the farm, and follow the track towards the corner of Low Wood. Just before reaching the wood, turn uphill alongside, and to left of, the

Wastwater with Yewbarrow, Kirkfell and Great Gable on the horizon

stream gully of Greathall Gill.

At the ridge-top, a path leads left, above the crags of the Screes, and past the summits of Whin Rigg and Illgill Head. There are fine views in all directions – including downwards, onto Wastwater...

From Illgill Head descend north-east, on steep grass, into a wide col. Ahead is the wide, high slope of Scafell. Keep to the left edge for an easier path and views down over Scafell Crag. Finally, turn right for 200yds across a stony plateau to Scafell's summit cairn.

SCAFELL

In the Lakes Threethousands chapter we've described the descents by Foxes Tarn and by Broad Stand. Failing the rock climb of Broad Stand, the most romantic route down is by the West Wall Traverse. Return across the stony plateau (north-east) to reach the top of Scafell Crag. The knoll of Symond's Knott will be on the left: the twin points of Scafell Pinnacle and Pisgah on the right. Directly below is Deep Gill. The gully is entered down a well-scuffed gravelly groove.

Descend the gully bed for 200ft (60m vertical), until another gully joins from the right – this is Professor's Chimney. Here look out for a cairn on the left, which marks the start of a path traversing out along a rocky ledge. It is most important not to descend the gully beyond this point. If the stones in the gully bed do not appear well-turned by many feet, you have gone down too far and are about to encounter overhanging rock-pitches.

The ledge path is the West Wall Traverse. It slants down among the crags, to reach the top of another gully that descends to the right. This gully too is floored with loose rocks.

At the foot of the gully, traverse to the right on a path below crags, to reach the eroded ground below Mickledore. Go up steeply to the pass.

A cairned path leads up the boulderfield to the summit of Scafell Pike. Do not sit down: almost anywhere on this walk is more exciting than that crowded cairn. So stop long enough only to ascertain the correct path off. This is the big one running north-east towards (eventually) Langdale. The all-rock top of Broad Crag is worth the short diversion. The boulder-hop to Ill Crag is worthwhile only if you plan to have lunch there: Ill Crag is excellent for picnics.

The path dips into the col before Great End, and can be followed for another 200yds into Calf Cove for the sake of the stream water. Then head up onto Great End. From its northernmost summit cairn, an interesting ridge descends directly to Sty Head Pass. The ridge has rocky bits, which can be climbed down or circumvented.

STY HEAD

The start of the Gable Traverse can be awkward to find – it is the smallest of the six paths leaving Sty Head. It climbs briefly beside a small stream, then heads left to pass below the small, clean crag of Kern Knotts. This flat face with its two cracks has been a classic testing-ground for rock climbers.

The path crosses the screes of Great Hell Gate, to reach the broken ground below the Nape's Buttresses. The Nape's Needle is just above, its shape unfamiliar because it's foreshortened. Pass below it, and go up to its base on a small scree.

The Climbers' Traverse now passes along the base of the rock climbs. The way is well scratched, a grade I scramble. The rock-pinnacle of the Sphinx appears on the skyline ahead, and the route passes immediately behind it, then descends on large holds.

Cross the shifting stones of Little Hell Gate scree, and traverse on among small outcrops, dropping slightly to reach a small path that has been below you all around the scrambling bits. The path crosses the wide screes of Gavel Neese, with cairns, to the col of Beck Head. There's a small spring at the point where the path arrives on the col.

A wide path leads up Kirk Fell, with scrambling on its left if preferred. From the second and higher summit, iron fence posts lead down the rocky spur to the Black Sail pass. A path leads on towards Pillar, skirting to left of the minor summit of Looking Stead to a flat ridge beyond.

Where the ridge steepens and becomes rocky, go up for just 20yds to a sprawling cairn. Here look round right for the start of a small path traversing across the steep and somewhat craggy slope. This is the famous Pillar High-Level Path. It dips and rises to avoid crags, and reaches the conical Robinson's Cairn. Here Pillar Rock leaps out from round the corner and hits you between the eyes.

The cairn commemorates John Wilson Robinson, whose winter trip round the Threethousands is described in the History chapter. It was he who invented this splendid way of getting to Pillar Rock; he climbed the Rock itself a hundred and one times. His friends raised the cairn in a storm on Easter Saturday 1908.

Cross the floor of the grassy combe beyond, and turn left up a gentle rock rib. Now the rock buttress of the Shamrock is on the right. A scree path runs up to left of it. At the top of the scree turn right, along the top of the buttress, on a rock shelf below overhangs. This is the Shamrock Traverse, which slants up to reach a scree amphitheatre directly opposite the Rock itself. Circle the top of the amphitheatre to reach the col between the Rock and the main mountain.

The nearest of Pillar Rock's pinnacles is Pisgah, and it may be reached by a short, exposed scramble on good rock (grade 1). Beyond Pisgah, the deep Jordan Gap prevents access to the main summit of High Man. Return to the col.

The slope of the main mountain, behind the col, may be ascended directly, with short scrambles on easy but slightly loose rock. Or there is a zig-zag path.

The summit of Pillar has a stone-built trig point. The descent routes are not visible from the flat summit: follow cairns south-west to find the rocky spur that descends to Wind Gap. A clear, rough path leads up Great Scoat Fell. Keep to the right of the summit wall for the views, and to find the short but very sharp ridge leading out to Steeple.

Return along the sharp ridge, and follow the wall to the right. Gentle grassy ground leads down to a col, and up onto Haycock. Turn left at the cairn to descend Haycock's south ridge: on the way down

Approaching Pillar Rock on the high-level traverse

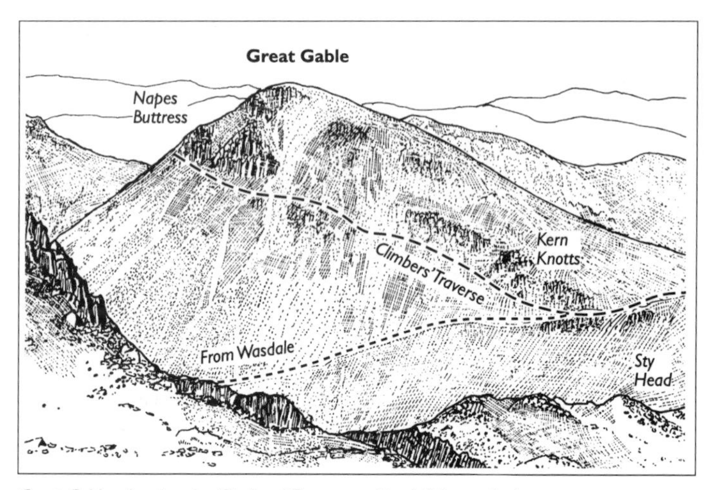

Great Gable, showing the Climbers' Traverse raking left beneath the crags

you may find yourself on a short rock-pitch of slabs and jumbled boulders. Small streams cross the wide col below.

The face of Seatallan is steep scree, but the north-east ridge, on the left, provides an easy ascent. Seatallan is a rounded hill, made of the Eskdale granite, but the view eastwards is utterly rough. Let a wisp of cloud cover the familiar shape of Mickledore, take a photo eastwards, and puzzle your friends with a place that must be rugged Ardgour, or maybe Knoydart – could that unfamiliar pointed peak be Sgurr na Ciche? Well no; it's Gable, seen from an unexpected direction – but taken with Yewbarrow, and Red Pike, and the Scafells, it provides a picture with not a smooth grassy slope anywhere.

A steep descent just south of east leads to the wide col above Greendale Tarn – you could drop to the tarn and go down to right of its stream for a quicker exit from the walk. But Middle Fell is better, if you're not yet tired of rocky landscape. Apart from its foreground outcrops, it offers a splendid view of the head of Wastwater. A faint path leads down its south-west ridge.

At the ridge foot the path reaches the brink of Greendale Gill. Here it meets a wider path, marked as right-of-way on the map. Go straight across this, and down steeply to the stream. This is crossed just above a small waterfall. The stream bed displays the pale, rounded rocks of the Eskdale granite. Slant up left, through bracken, to find a path just above a solitary holly tree. This path descends to the left, below the crag face of Buckbarrow, to reach the minor road at Buckbarrow farm.

Go through the farm, turning right onto a walled track. Where the track ends, follow the wall on the left for 200yds to a signpost. Here the bridleway (to be used) on the left is clearer than the ill-defined footpath ahead. It follows the field edge, with a wall on its right, to cross a small stream after 200yds.

The bridleway is now a grassy track that bends right to a small stone bridge. Keep straight ahead across a narrow field to another signpost. The forward finger is marked 'Strands'.

Follow wall on the left to reach a stony track. All this may be ordinary field-edge walking, but it is given a special atmosphere by the high rock walls of Buckbarrow and the Screes hemming it in on either side. The track leads through a farm to rejoin the road at the crossroads just east of Nether Wasdale.

A Caldew Circuit

In various guide books we read of the delicious solitude to be found at the Back o' Skiddaw.

If you go to a party and there's nobody else about you don't, of course, congratulate yourself on the peace and quiet. You wonder what it is that makes your host so desperately uncool, and leave.

So what's wrong with the Back o' Skiddaw? From the top o' Skiddaw you see greeny-brown rolling hills. There are surprisingly many of them, given that you can actually name only two high points north of the A66 (and you're standing on one of the two already). The map says they're over 2000ft, which ought to make them count as mountains.

Mountains, however, they are not; and that greeny-brown colour tells us why. Here is peat bog instead of frost-shattered rock. Here is heather where it should be crag. This small corner has been invaded by a bit of the Rest of England, or possibly of Scotland's Southern Uplands. This is the stuff people who can't get to the Lakes have to walk over: people who walk Yorkshire, or Bowland, or the Cheviots, while congratulating themselves on the delicious solitude and trying to forget that it's because the other hillwalkers are all on Bowfell or Steeple.

My first steps into the Back o' Skiddaw were on the Bob Graham run. I liked the heather-slopes of Great Calva, though my reasons for doing so were rather artificial. Just in front, a party from Ambleside was having trouble doing deep heather in the dark, and I wasn't. I come from the Southern Uplands, and deep heather's what I usually run in.

Later, having passed my boots over most of Lakeland proper, I looked again at the River Caldew. Back o' Skiddaw is actually closer to home than the Cheviots: why not do a day of Southern Upland walking in the Lakes?

I went expecting little, and was pleasantly surprised. This may be the worst of Lakeland, but bad Lakeland is as good as the best of everywhere else. I found a classic tarn, in a rocky hollow of the traditional sort, but without picnickers. I found four deep-slotted valleys to cross. I found a perfectly adequate waterfall. Several of the ridges were neither heathery nor tussocky. And though Knott was not exciting, Carrock Fell gave as rough and stony an ending as any of those beastly descents into Langdale.

Add Blencathra (not at the Back o' Skiddaw on anybody's map) for a day that's not nearly so bad as all that. And then, there's all that delicious solitude...

Start/finish: Mosedale/Bowscale, north of Mungrisedale. Note: Limited parking on verges at the bridge over the Caldew, and south of Bowscale.
20 miles, 7500ft (32km, 2300m)
Map: Landranger 30 (Penrith) or Harveys Lakeland North

A bridleway sign indicates a rough track on the left at the southern entrance to Bowscale hamlet. The track climbs gradually up the side of the Caldew valley, giving a good view of the rather large river whose watershed we plan to walk. It also gives a view of the descent path off Carrock Fell, the one you're going to be unable to find the top of in ten or twelve hours from now...

The track climbs to the outflow of Bowscale Tarn. This was a favourite one in Victorian times, and it's easy to see why. It's a dark crag-hung water as featured in geography texts, and though the gentle walk in is less than two miles, it has cleverly turned a corner. Thus, from the tarn, you look out at much more than two miles of uninhabitable steep slopes.

The green path continues along the left side of the tarn, then slants up to the right above its head. As it bends to return above the west side of the tarn it starts to slope down; here leave it and head straight up a steep grass slope. When crags block the way upwards, slant up right – this is rather steep, with a view between your knees down to the dark waters. Soon though, you reach the gentle grassy ridge above Tarn Crags. Go straight up to the summit of Bowscale Fell.

Descend slightly west of south into a flat boggy col. The path continues slantwise out of the col without change of direction to the lower col at the head of the Glenderamackin (GR 327292), but it's worth turning up left to visit the summit of Bannerdale Crags. Or rather, to visit the cairn 200yds east of the summit: for this lower cairn is perched at the edge of the crags and shows what excitements are lurking just under the rim of the grass. Return westwards, following the top of steep ground on the left, to pick up a path into that same col at the head of the Glenderamackin.

From here a path down left leads to the Scale Beck, for those who want to include Sharp Edge (which is described in the 'Four and More' chapter on page 72). Otherwise go straight up out of the col on a clear path. There are fine views across to Sharp Edge. When the path reaches the plateau, continue south, through a dip with a puddle-tarn.

The summit cairn is beside a concrete ring, where surveying instruments were mounted in days when incredulous surveyors were confirming that Blencathra does not, in fact, achieve three thousand feet. Continue south-west, with the drops and various plunging ridges on

Bowscale Tarn

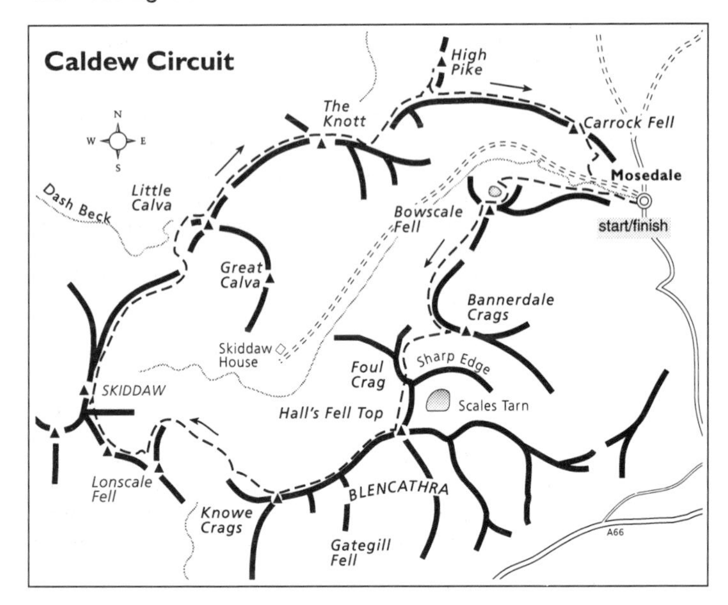

the left, to the end of the plateau at Knowe Crags. Go down, slightly north of west, to the track in the bottom of the Glenderaterra Valley.

This is a big place. The high spire of Lonscale Fell rears above, and the long slopes of Skiddaw and Blencathra lie back behind, to give a view through into the wide, empty place that is the head of the Caldew.

Turn right up the track, which crosses the beck at a wooden footbridge, climbs for 300yds and bends right – it's heading towards the youth hostel at Skiddaw House. Stay on the track for 200yds after the bend, then turn up left onto the slopes, at this point bracken-free, of Burnt Horse. At the top a fence guides along the top of small crags into a col. Slant up left, to reach the plateau close to the 703m spot-height at the east end of Lonscale Fell. This point, poised above the Glenderamackin, deserves to be the hill's summit.

Return to the fence corner and cross a stile to reach the actual summit, a nondescript small cairn in a sheep-field. At the fence junction 100yds beyond, a gate leads through the westward fence to a path. Path and fence lead over Jenkin Hill to the main Keswick-

Skiddaw path. Go downhill through the gate on this path, then up the slope opposite, to Little Man. A large path leads on to the summit of Skiddaw.

The ridge continuing northwards is quiet – indeed, 'deliciously solitary', as we are here entering the Back o' Skiddaw. Accordingly, the ground turns from stones to grass. A long, gentle descent with fence alongside leads to the track at the top of the Whitewater Dash. You can scramble down below the main track for various vertical looks down the waterfalls: if your walking companion happens also to be a deadly enemy, this would be the place for the final life-and-death struggle. Otherwise, turn uphill for a few steps to go through the gate on the main track, then cross the Dash Beck to go up the slope opposite alongside the fence. A small path helps slightly through the heather. At the top the fence bends right at a stile – don't cross it, but continue to right of the fence across the rough summit of Little Calva.

The fence leads onwards to a stile at a right bend. Cross this one, and go forward on pathless wet heather to the col. The ground becomes pleasantly grassy, and a quad-bike path leads up to the summit of Knott. Here, to my surprise, I passed another hillwalker: I don't say 'met', as the man circled the cairn and strode away briskly, clearly both a Wainwright-bagger and a solitude seeker. I gave him my surliest glance so as not to spoil his misanthropic pleasure.

From Knott, a short descent eastward leads to a boggy col, but firm ground is found again on the low eminence of Iron Crag. After Great Lingy Hill a gravel track joins from the right – this is the line marked as 'Cumbria Way'. With still two hours left of daylight, I was tempted to wander up the grassy slope onto High Pike. This is off the watershed and makes me too a mere Wainwright-bagger, but there is a stone bench at the summit, from which to admire the Solway, distant Scottish Criffel and the sunset clouds, all pink-and-orange on Skiddaw. Apart from the tips of the Grasmoor group, none of the central fells are visible, and it was hard to believe I was just ten miles from Keswick.

A good grassy path leads back down to the Cumbria Way track. If light is fading, follow this track back to the right for an easy descent to the Caldew – the final drop off Carrock Fell is not one to attempt by torchlight. For those not threatened by the coming of the night, the path continues across the track and along the ridge to Carrock Fell. The ground here has small but enjoyable rocky outcrops, and the summit itself is a pile of pink granite. The slope beyond is the edge of the Lake District, geologically speaking, though the Park boundary is a

Bannerdale Crags, seen here from Souther Fell

further mile out into the plain. Nowhere, not even on Black Coombe, can you stand so high with the edge of the flat country right at your feet.

Leave Carrock Fell on a bearing of 145°, down a long slope of short heather. The final ridge-end has a cairn: just before this, a small scree path zig-zags down the right-hand flank. It passes through ankle-scratching gorse: but your ankles suffer far worse if you are unlucky and miss the path.

Turn left, along the small tarred road, to Mosedale.

Across Lakeland
From Penrith to the Sea

Just Passing By

You don't have to get high to have fun. This applies to Lakeland as much as to any depraved habits of the club scene! Following this principle, we attempted to get all the way across, from Penrith to the sea, without crossing a single mountain. While by-passing summit cairns we passed lakesides, crossed passes, and took the pasture paths.

1998 was the year of the duck: the British summer had not managed to string together more than two consecutive days of sunshine for those of us in the North of England. Consequently, as John and I set off on our journey to Penrith, our expectations of bad weather were so high that all the contents of our rucksacks had to be wrapped in polythene bags – and even the polythene bags had to be wrapped in polythene bags.

Our trip began in the aisles of Safeway's, not the most inspiring of places when the mountains are so close at hand. Still it gave John and me a chance to reminisce about our previous backpacking exploits on the Snowdonia to Gower route. "No wonder our rucksacks weighed 60 and 70lb when we were carrying tins of Irish stew and cans of beer," I remarked. "Still, our years of experience have taught us the art of back-packing light now." John nodded in agreement as he placed four bottles of Australian Chardonnay in the trolley.

To save time we decided to start from Askham. We hoisted the bulging rucksacks onto our backs and strode vigorously out of the village. "I feel a bit like the hunchback of Notre Dame wearing this thing," I said to John. "The fells, the fells," he cried, pointing towards the mountains. John's repertoire of bad jokes gives new meaning to the concept of endurance walking.

We strolled across Moor Divock looking back on the sprawling mass of Penrith and the dark Pennine hills beyond. If we had looked forward instead we might have noticed that the path had suddenly disappeared from beneath our feet. We stood staring at the moors and wondered why none of the paths we could see matched those on the map. "What did you do last time you were here?" John inquired. " Oh, I got lost then too," I replied. We knew the general direction and after a few minutes of bracken slaying we were back on course.

It was a lovely sunny evening and as Ullswater came into view we started to look forward to a wild campsite. Alas, with the heat comes the midge and I had foolishly worn my shorts. I slapped my thighs and legs like a Bavarian entertainer as the little blithers began their relentless attack. I had read in one of Ronald's books that splattering the midge is the worst thing that you can do as it spreads the infection. However I had the consolation of knowing that it was certainly the worst thing for the midge as well. John pointed out that it was only the female mosquitoes that were biting me. Gosh, he must have good eyesight!

I convinced John that we had an obligation to check out the facilities for our readers, and drew his attention to the inn at Howton. John, as a scrupulous researcher, agreed. I had passed the Howton Inn in January but found it closed. The publican, who was standing outside it, suggested I could wait, if I wasn't in a hurry, until it opened. I asked when that would be. "March," he chuckled as he went inside.

What the Howton Inn lacks in size it makes up for in character, and we spent a pleasant half hour among the horse brasses and antique fittings of the walkers' bar. It was getting dark by the time we found near Geordies Crag a patch of green just big enough for our tent. We eagerly broke out the Chardonnay and picked the highest rock to admire the view from. John pointed out the Sharrow Bay restaurant: "Ronald says you can get a really nice meal there if you've got a spare fifty quid." Hardened fellrunners shouldn't know about such things.

While we chatted the sun went down behind Gowbarrow Fell and the flickering lights of Howton appeared beneath the blackness of Hallin Fell. A short while later they were outshone by a million stars that filled the night sky. When the cool breeze became too uncomfortable we slipped into our cosy sleeping bags. It had been a perfect start to our walk.

The next day the tent was unzipped to reveal a beautiful sunny morning. We marvelled at our excellent choice of campsite. Ullswater lay before us big and fat and we were surrounded by rugged crags. Neither of fancied cooking anything more adventurous than coffee, so we made a lazy breakfast of Muller rice and cereal bars. It was then we realised that the buzzing we could hear was not the effects of the Chardonnay from the previous night, but a nest of bees that we had set up camp beside. This disturbed John because he had just had a nasty experience in Austria. Chances are that if you saw a yodeller running through the Alps faster than Linford Christie last year, then that was John being hotly pursued by an angry swarm. So we swiftly packed and began our second day's walking.

It was not long before we felt the first spots of rain, quickly followed by lashings of fine wetting drizzle, although the trees kept most of the rain from us to start with. I recalled my last walk here in the winter when greasy twisted tree roots were covered by wet leaves on the lakeside path. That was a gloomy day accompanied only by the lapping of the grey waters of Ullswater against the rocky shoreline.

We made a detour to Patterdale in the hope of a cup of tea, but settled for a can of pop and a Mars bar from the village shop. We were reluctant to leave the comforts of Patterdale as the rain was getting heavier and a thick mist clung firmly to the mountains. As we strode along the woodland paths beside Brotherswater we could see the Scandale Pass for miles ahead, and we knew exactly what was in store for us. There was a short break while we waited for the rangers to finish constructing the footbridge near Hartsop Hall, but Scandale could not be put off any longer.

We scrambled over the slimy lichen-coated rocks of the Scandale path. The water that followed the course of the path soon found its way into John's air-conditioned boots, which had served him so well. As we neared the top of the pass two shadows appeared out of the swirling mist. It was August, the peak of the season, and these were the first walkers we had met.

After crossing the wall at the pass top conditions improved from very bad to merely horrible. No longer was the rain being driven into our eyes and forced up our nostrils although the air was still damp and weighed heavy on our lungs. The grim shadows of the crags that sheltered us from those wild winds were softened by the thick mists. Ambleside was downhill, but several miles of raw valley and wind-stretched trees separated us from it. The only highlight was the ancient packhorse bridge at the bottom.

Ambleside with its many cafes and walking shops gets busy in the rain and the narrow crowded pavements are no place for heavily laden

Roy getting drenched at High Sweden Bridge on the descent into Ambleside

backpackers. John and I managed to find a quiet space – next to the bar in the Queens Head. There we carefully unfolded our soggy map and studied it for campsites. The rain had lashed us forward and our intended choice of Loughrigg was now too close, while Coniston was too far away.

Once you stop in the wet it is hard to get started again and the steep windy roads to Loughrigg were painfully slow. We splashed through the puddles on the cart track that traversed the fell top. Not another soul had braved the elements on this normally popular hill.

On the road near Skelwith we encountered another peril as speeding cars pinned us to the hedgerows. Still, what they pinned us to were blackberries, a tasty appetiser to the evening meal we had promised ourselves at the Skelwith Bridge hotel.

We arrived at the hotel twenty minutes before opening time. Peering through the glass we noted that it looked quite posh inside – and we didn't. We thought there might be objections to us spreading lumps of Loughrigg on their carpet, so we decided to change into dry clothes. The change had to be quick, both to avoid getting wet and to avoid getting arrested. We sheltered under the porch watching the rain pour from the guttering to form pools on the plastic tables and chairs. Once inside we hung our dripping cagoules on the stand and feasted on Cumberland sausage and chips washed down with a couple of pints of Ruddles. This holiday was turning into a bit of a pub crawl.

It was not a pleasant experience changing back into damp boots and cold wet cagoules. There was also a feeling of overindulgence, though our bloated stomachs now countered the weight of our rucksacks.

Under tree cover the bad weather meant that darkness came quicker than expected. The maps were barely readable and we had to resort to torches. The torrents of Colwith Force could be heard but not seen, and paths criss-crossed in all directions. Water fell from the trees by the bucket load as we fought the low branches of pine trees in search of the way out. As we paced around in fast angry circles, we suddenly spotted the gate at the edge of the wood.

We began looking for a place to set up the tent and our standards were falling by the minute. We slipped through a gate into a marshy field and found a bit of ground that was fairly flat and out of sight of any farmhouses. The tent pegs went in easily, too easily for my liking, but all I wanted to do was get out of the rain and get horizontal and forget this awful experience.

It continued to rain hard through the night and most of the water found its way into the tent. Our sleeping bags were wet and so were our clothes, but it was a warm comfortable wet in spite of the contortions the grassy lumps had enforced. Neither of us wanted to venture outside the tent, but neither did we fancy waiting in to meet an irate farmer. Mind you it wasn't a place where farmers would think of looking for discourteous campers – only the most desperate of walkers (or a Scottish fellrunner) would have been crazy enough to float his tent in the middle of a peat bog. Indeed, any respectable farmer would be too embarrassed to admit ownership of such a field.

As we set off we noticed the patches of blue sky that meant all the rain was now packed in our rucksacks and there was none left in the sky. Early morning on the quiet roads bought us into contact with the local wildlife and in only a few hundred yards we had seen squirrels, a fox, deer, and a flat hedgehog. Knitting together roadside footpaths we reached Coniston in time for a late breakfast. A couple of bacon sandwiches and a mug of tea and we were ready to tackle the shopping. Walna Scar was a different matter.

Yesterday we had complained about the rain, today we complained about the sun, which made carrying heavy packs up the Walna Scar road hard work. The glorious Coniston fells provided some consolation and John asked me to take a photo of him with his camera. "It's fool-proof; just point and press," he shouted. I pointed, pressed, and was most surprised to see the back of the camera fly open. "Call that fool-proof, then, John," I laughed. No ordinary foolproofing can withstand the Clayton Finger.

We arrived at Seathwaite at the same time as a minibus crammed with Japanese tourists so we had to wait at the bar while they observed the English tradition of afternoon tea and biscuits. We then observed our own tradition – a pint and a packet of crisps, much nicer. This was the last pub of the journey, so it was with sadness that we bade farewell to our friendly host and set off towards the little, and little-visited, Dunnerdale fells.

We found a spot near the top of Caw to pitch our tent. After two and a half days without a bath I looked forward to bathing in the refreshing waters of the nearby stream. The icy waters soon shrivelled my enthusiasm (as well as various other bits). Back in the tent John had made hot chocolate. As we sipped our drinks and commented on how peaceful Dunnerdale was, half a dozen scrambling bikes suddenly whizzed down the track.

Neither of us had ever visited this odd corner of Lakeland. On the

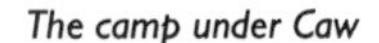
The camp under Caw

maps it looked rocky and interesting, but this had not fully prepared us for the intricate beauty of miniature craggy knolls and fun-size boulders that childhood dreams are made of. Without our rucksacks we felt almost weightless and free to run to the tops effortlessly. While we explored every inch of our new playground the red sun began to set over another idyllic campsite.

We woke and were pleased to see the sun still shining on what would be our last day. Ten minutes walking and we could see the Duddon estuary, our intended destination. On the map, what looked like an ideal path led towards Broughton Mills. When we found it we were disappointed. Barbed wire positioned at eye level threatened serious injury. I did not fancy being barbed, so we decided to hack our own course through the tall bracken. Next time we would try a route past Stickle Tarn.

We were eager to finish but the field paths around Broughton Mills were complicated and time-consuming. A buzzard swooped from the trees to entertain us with an exhibition of flying skills. John suggested it might be a vulture waiting for the demise of two flagging walkers, so we picked up the pace and pretended as hard as we could to be still alive.

We had already decided not to go over Black Coombe, so were gratified to see that Black Coombe was under depressing black cloud. Perhaps we might be due one more soaking before the finish. We could see the estuary, but there was a noticeable lack of signposts. The inhabitants of Lady Hall looked out of their windows bemused as two walkers and their rucksacks became entangled in the sheets, towels and nappies hanging from their washing lines. A young boy came out to point the way through a well-concealed rusty gate.

Soon we were on the Duddon Estuary looking across to Broughton and Barrow-in-Furness. The first mile was nice, the second was not so nice, and by the third mile of the endless flat green embankment we were counting off field-edges against the map. We could see the spire of Millom church but it never got any closer. We had also run out of drinks, with the exception of some very suspect mossy water from the previous day. (Don't worry: I came back later to work out a better ending.)

Eventually we did reach Millom, and changed into dry clothes on a bench outside the town. We had low expectations of Millom, and we were not disappointed. The town, built around the mining industry, seemed to be struggling for an identity since the decline of shipbuilding. Its boarded up shop windows and graffiti were interestingly different from the delights of Askham, Ambleside, Patterdale and Coniston.

"The future of Millom is in tourism," a billboard exclaimed. "I think the future of Millom is in glazing," I said to John.

It was 5pm and the town was closing, so we headed for the railway station. The station matched its village – locked doors, dusty windows, a waiting room turned diner and a platform that had become a meeting place for bored youths.

From the train we were treated to a spectacular sunset over the Isle of Man and the Scottish Lowlands. It was a reminder of those brilliant nights at Ullswater and Duddon, and could almost erase the painful memory of our bog bed near Colwith Force. Through the right-hand windows, night gathered in the hollow of Eskdale, and the Grasmoor hills became a few faint lines against the sky. Finally Lakeland faded into darkness; and then they came up the train with the drinks trolley.

FROM PENRITH OVER THE PASSES

50 miles low-level across Lakeland

Do spirits necessarily drop with altitude? In the Lake District, anyway, the answer is no. Arguably the nicest five miles in Cumbria is the northern shore of Ullswater. The country between Ambleside, Coniston and the bottom end of Langdale is oakwoods, stone roads between high walls, and waterfalls. And under the showers of Spring, the Summer downpour, the Autumn mists or the Winter blizzard, the

Descending Moor Divock towards Ullswater

achievement of a high pass gives you just enough nastiness to be interesting before letting you back down to the shelter of the trees.

Here, then, is a fifty-mile (80km) walk from Penrith to the sea that includes two high passes, a couple of tarns, quite a few oakwoods and waterfalls, and that Ullswater path. It's a walk that is enjoyable every step of the way, and gives the lie to the assertion that a walk has to be high-level to be high-quality. As a bonus, the avoidance of those not-altogether-enjoyable steep uphills, as well as of those perhaps-even-less-enjoyable steep downs, lets you get all the way across Cumbria within the limits of a rather long long weekend.

Take a tent, by all means, if you like uncomfortable nights and early-morning starts. Or travel fast and light, and lie in till late between the soft sheets of Brotherswater and Dunnerdale. Every few miles along the route there are places with beds in, places to cook you a meal, and places selling beer.

So forget for a while the frigid ridges and the depressing elevations. No more moping on slopes! Take your ease among the trees and enjoy a high old time on the low-level route.

Start: Penrith railway station
Finish: Foxfield railway station
45 miles, 7100ft (72km 2100 m)
Map: Landrangers 90 (Penrith) and 96 (Barrow); or Outdoor Leisure Maps 5, 6 and 7 (No 6 needs to be the new double-sided one)

1: Penrith to Patterdale: 15 miles/24km

The start is deliberately low-key: a country town with a pink castle, a riverside, and a grassy limestone moor. All this is pleasant enough, until at the edge of Moor Divock you suddenly find yourself surrounded by something much pleasanter: real mountains. The Ullswater path is a delight.

Walk out of Penrith railway station and under a sandstone arch into Castle Park. The ruined Penrith Castle is on the left. It was built by William Strickland in 1399 and was later the home of the Duke of Gloucester, who became Richard III.

Follow the tarmac pathway past a bandstand to the park's exit. Cross to a path between some houses and at the street beyond turn left for 40yds. Then head right along a road past the Ullswater

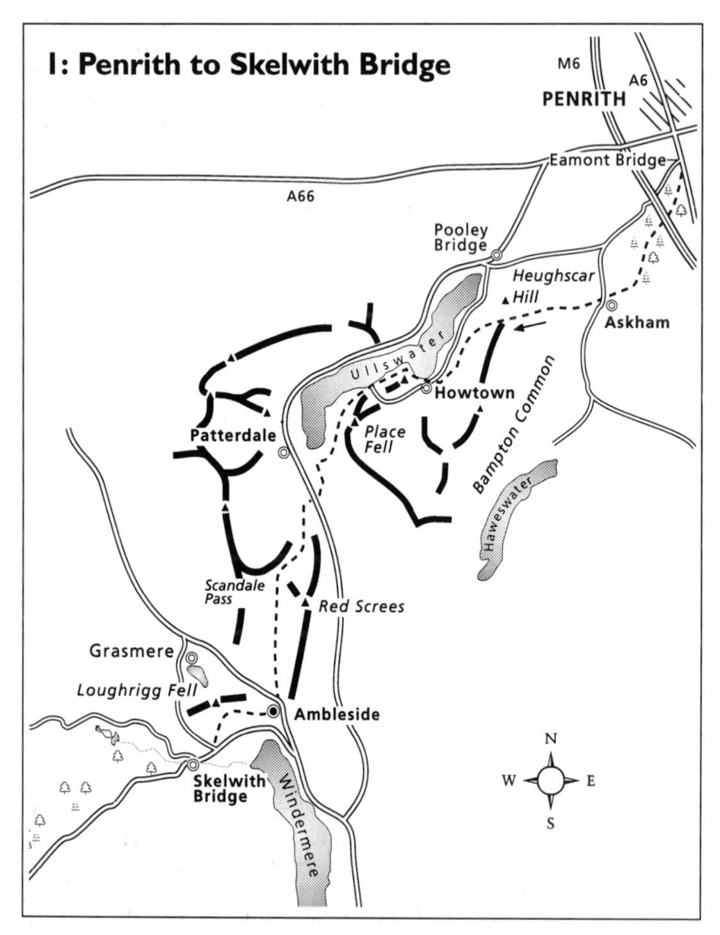

Education Institute. After 600yds the street bends right but a footpath runs forward to the A66 roundabout. Pick a spot between the juggernauts and dart across the road to where a path down on the right leads to the more sedate village of Eamont Bridge.

Resist the temptation of the two inns positioned either side of the road. At the end of the village is King Arthur's Round Table. This is a remnant of the Neolithic Age and not where King Arthur and his nobles picnicked al fresco. Follow the A6 to Lowther Park Holiday Centre on the bend 200yds beyond. The remarkably straight road known as Earl Henry's Drive with its regimented pines runs parallel to the River Lowther, passing underneath the M6 and then a railway viaduct to reach the caravan site.

Go through the gate into the caravan park to a second gate at the far end. A woodland track now returns to the river and runs alongside it to Low Gardens Bridge. Just prior to the bridge, turn right through an iron kissing gate and begin a steep ascent on a pleasant woodland trail. The steepness is short-lived, as are the woods, the path emerging via a ladder stile into an open field. We have now crossed the boundary into the Lake District National Park proper.

The classy bit of stone-work on the left is Askham Hall, the residence of the Earl of Lonsdale. Slant diagonally left across a field to a bridleway. A left turn along the lane will bring you to Askham (Place of the Ashes).

Askham seems like a Pennine village with its little limestone cottages arranged neatly along the village green. Two pubs, the Punchbowl and the 17th-century Queens Head, are renowned for good food and ale.

Turn right, through the village, to a T-junction by the village store, and go along the cul-de-sac opposite, keeping right at a fork. This road rises moderately as it aims for the open fells. After 400yds the path peels off, and the left side of the dry-stone wall is traced. In retrospect

First night's camp at Geordie's Crag, Ullswater

the sprawling mass of Penrith and the rather regal Lowther Castle are backed by the dark Pennines.

Moor Divock is a network of paths, and strict adherence to the bridleway line involves some bracken bashing (or the other way round). Instead aim for the copse at Riggingleys Top and, just short of the trees, take the easy path to the left (slightly south of west).

You'll reach a four-way signpost at Ketley Gate (GR 487225). Go straight on for 400yds to find the Cockpit stone circle. The wiggles of Ullswater can now be seen below; further back, Blencathra and Sharp Edge are prominent.

The path gets a little too squishy on the approach to Aik Beck, where it drops into the recess and climbs back out beside a signpost showing the way to Howtown. Now the way is a clear path, although there's still some rugged landscape to be admired on the left as we pass below Auterstone Crag on the lower flanks of Bonscale and Arthur's Pikes.

After two miles (3km) Howtown pier can be seen through the trees. The track passes above a cottage with a static caravan. (Howtown village can be bypassed by taking a path that goes down to left of this caravan, descending to cross a road to the pier.) To take in the village, continue on the main track to Mellguards, then descend through a gate on the right. A public footpath (signposted) avoids a short private drive, and crosses a clapper bridge before turning right to the Howton Inn. During the peak season the village is the destination of tourists from Patterdale travelling by one of the two steamers (diesel ones), the 'Lady of the Lake' and the 'Raven'.

At the end of the pub driveway a path 'to Sandwick' runs to the lake, then begins a steep climb of 50yds on earth steps, turning right at the top by a line of trees. After passing Geordie's Crags the path curves left to enter Hallinhag Woods. The oak, beech, alder, birch and rowan trees of Kailpot Crag frame some marvellous views across the water to the promontory of Skelly Nab – the Skelly is a type of freshwater herring that can only be found in Ullswater.

This is the second longest of the lakes, and one of the deepest with a maximum depth of 205ft. A speed limit of 10mph imposed in 1983 has restored some of the serene qualities that Windermere and Coniston lack. The lake had in the past been used as a venue for attempts on speed records.

After running above a sandy cove, the smallest and least radioactive of Cumbrian beaches, the path crosses a pasture into Sandwick. Turn left for 25yds, then take the bridleway rising to the right alongside a wall. Route description is not necessary as a proliferation of 'Private' notices shepherds you quickly out of the hamlet.

The next point of interest is Scalehow Force, a splendid waterfall slithering down the eastern side of Place Fell. Cross the footbridge at the foot of the falls and begin climbing again. Although this is a lake-side path it is by no means flat. A thousand feet of height are lost and gained along Ullswater side, while greasy, twisted tree roots attempt to catch you unaware. At Silver Point grey outcrops of rock and juniper berries provide foreground for lake photos. Some small islands are dotted close to the shoreline. The largest of these is Norfolk Island, famous for its bird-life (but not turkeys).

Patterdale soon comes into view. Multi-coloured yachts glide across the lake beside steamers, and white-washed cottages and pubs nestle beneath crinkled knolls on the lower slopes of Helvellyn. For those who wish to experience the swinging night-life of Patterdale, there is a convenient track to the village from Side Farm. Patterdale is thought to have acquired its name from St Patrick who was shipwrecked on Duddon Sands in AD540 – demonstrating the importance of carrying a compass. The village has shops, hotels and a youth hostel.

2: Patterdale to Ambleside: 9 miles/14km

After three miles along the floor of the deep valley comes the first pass crossing. At 1680ft the Scandale Pass is not the highest, but it is the bleakest point of the walk. A smooth easy path soon brings you down to the trees again, and to the busy town of Ambleside.

Looking ahead from Side Farm the route to the Scandale Pass can be traced with the better known Kirkstone Pass to the left. The slopes here are high grass ones, and the peaks – Gray Crag, the Hartsop Dodds and Red Screes – are conical like a child's drawing. Almost at once the bridleway reaches tarred lane at Rooking. Turn right for 100yds, then keep ahead on a footpath that passes to left of Crookabeck. After a mile (1.5km) of pleasant woodland walking a junction of paths is reached. The lower path is signposted 'Deepdale Bridge', but we take the higher one that goes through a gate climbing briefly. After passing a new complex of log cabins, the path comes to a minor farm road to Hartsop: 'Valley of the Red Deer'. The parish dates back to the 12th Century.

Turn right, returning to the main Patterdale road at a telephone box, and go right again for a couple of minutes into the car park near the northern edge of Brotherswater. Go through a gate on the left into Low Wood and follow a wide path towards Hartsop Hall. The track runs alongside Brotherswater (named after two brothers who drowned here when skating).

At Hartsop Hall the path splits. Take the left path skipping between the wire fence and the nettles through a field to a footbridge. Go over the bridge and trace the wall on the right to Caiston Glen. The path then starts to rise steeply over slippery rocks to the Scandale Pass, becoming indistinct and marshy in places. There are some pleasant waterfalls in the gorge on the left-hand side of the valley. After some climbing the wall at the top of the pass is reached and crossed by a ladder stile.

Once on the other side we begin a gradual descent beneath the wing of Hart Crag. The weather-worn path reaches a gate after half a mile and the track follows the wall into a walled lane. High Sweden Bridge, a delightful little packhorse bridge, is seen on the right; our path merges with the track from it. Continue on the left bank of Scandale Beck underneath trees and past some quarries to Ambleside.

The town has two attractions worthy of a visit. The famous Bridge House, built over a river, is said to be a Scotsman's attempt to avoid paying ground rent. Now owned by the National Trust, it once housed an entire family.

The second attraction is the Stock Ghyll waterfall, a 60ft (20m) double cascade beautifully set in woodlands. This twenty-minute detour is particularly picturesque in the spring when the daffodils and bluebells are in bloom.

3: Ambleside to Coniston: 8 miles/13km

This is Lakeland's low country of woodlands, ancient roads and riversides. The little but extremely lumpy fell, Loughrigg, is followed by several woods, quite a few pubs, and a classic tarn.

Leave the town by way of the church of St Anne. Pass to right of the church and into the Rothay Park football fields. Go straight across the park (just north of west: this urban navigation can be the devil) to a stone bridge over the Rothay.

Turn right along the road for 30yds. Next take the steep road on the left, winding to Brow Head. Loughrigg is an intricate web of paths and it is surprisingly easy to get lost on this small hill. However if your map is Outdoor Leisure and your eyesight sharp enough for the pale brown contours, the Clappersgate path opposite the farm offers excellent views over the whole of Ambleside and rejoins our main route after about 1km. The easiest way is the main bridleway to the right, the continuation of the tarred lane. The rough track passes through two gates and bends left through bracken to meet a stream. As the track begins to descend there is a gate on the left and a path through two fields to the Loughrigg Tarn lane at GR 348038. Turn left to find the A593, then right for 400yds to Skelwith Bridge.

The ten-minute detour to Skelwith Force is worthwhile, especially after heavy rainfall. It squeezes a greater volume of water than any other Lakeland waterfall between two shallow walls of rock.

Head along the Coniston road for 75yds to the second of two public footpath signs on the right. The path climbs gently through a wood, then joins a more obvious farm track that has climbed from the road below left. This passes left of a farm, then traces the top edge of some woodland, before swinging left through the front yard of Park Farm. A waymarked path now crosses the driveway just south of Low Park and bears left across the next field to enter a wood above the river. It drops left through the trees to the Elterwater road.

Turn right for a short way to a footpath sign hiding in the trees. Take this path to the left, but immediately fork off right onto the lower path that looks down onto Colwith Force. This hard-to-photograph fall is a series of cascades which drop about 15m (45ft), split by a boulder at the base.

The path starts climbing again, and exits the woods via a gate to an open field with High Park (B&B) to the right of the dry-stone wall. Turn left up to a tarred lane, and left along this.

We have now rejoined the Cumbria Way, which we shall follow to Coniston. The road soon joins the A593. A footpath alongside the main road is signed 'Glen Mary's Bridge' and leads south to High Cross.

Cross the main road and follow a tarred track south-east up Hollin Bank. Where it bends left towards Arnside farms go straight ahead along a rough track. Keep alert for speeding mountain bikers. At a sharp left bend, a gate ahead leads into the woods around the head of Tarn Hows. A gravel path runs alongside the western shores to a footbridge dam at the tarn's foot.

Head for the car park above the lake and turn right along the road for 500yds, then take a right again along the lane for Tarn Hows Cottages. Just before the cottages a concessionary path turns back left alongside the front garden. It then slants down below the trees and

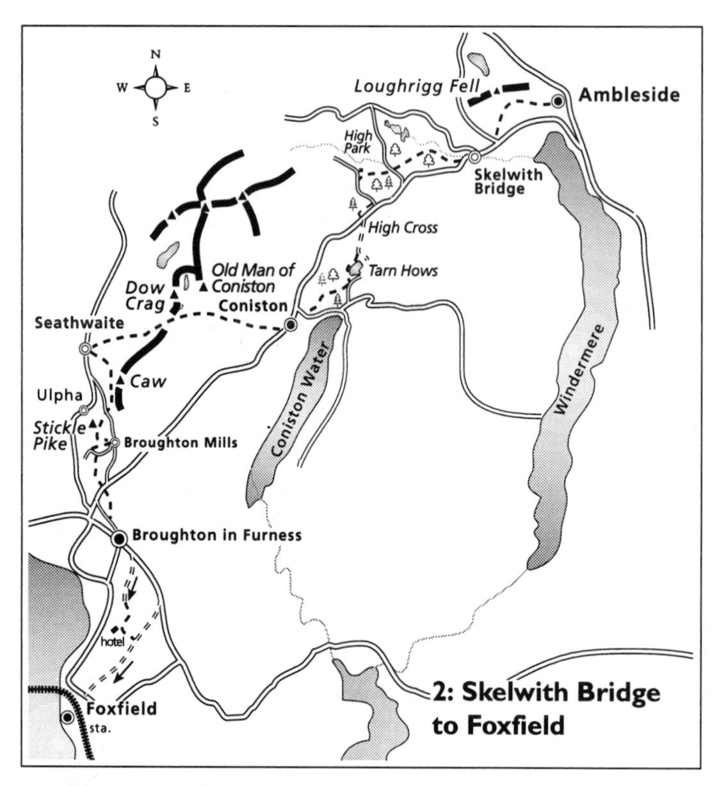

into Tarn Hows Woods. Cross a deer fence by a complicated stile and gate arrangement; then a path alongside a hedge leads to Low Yewdale.

Do not cross the bridge, but instead turn left for 200yds to a clump of trees. Negotiate a stile on the right marked 'Coniston and Cumbria Way', where an indistinct field path contours to the corner of a wood. The way keeps to the right of the wood, then passes under the trees. Go straight across the field beyond and descend through rampant gorse to the edge of Coniston. Once over Shepherds Bridge turn left, and back right at a second bridge to the town centre.

Coniston grew up and prospered around the copper industry, which once employed over nine hundred townsfolk. The relics of the mining days still litter the routes to Coniston Old Man, the mountain that dominates the region.

4: Coniston to Broughton Mills: 9 miles/15km

At well over half way, Coniston is the last town on the route and an essential re-supply point. The next objective is Walna Scar (605m/1990ft), the highest point of the walk. In sharp contrast to Scandale, this second pass offers wide views and an exposed ridge-top. The route then drops into the quiet, green valley of Duddon. Small rocky hills, visited by few, lead out to the southern plains.

Leave Coniston along the A593 in the direction of Torver, as far as the Ship pub. Behind the Ship a track rises steeply, crossing a disused railway line. Turn right then left before passing to the left of a farmhouse. A stony track beside a stream continues to rise and one last field brings you to a gate and the open fell. From the top of the stile a look back reveals the full length of Coniston Water. Sadly Coniston will always be associated with Donald Campbell, who died in 1967 attempting to break the water speed record.

A vague path continues straight ahead over rough grass and bracken to a beck, which it follows up to the stony Walna Scar road. Here in 1954 a schoolboy took one of the most convincing photographs ever of a UFO. Walna Scar has been a trade route used by shepherds, peddlers and weavers since Roman times, as well as for the transportation of copper to the harbour at Ravenglass.

The road is stony and rough, and becomes steep as it winds to the top of the pass. Rugged Harter Fell sits undaunted in the company of the entire Scafell range, with the Australian sounding Wallowbarrow Gorge cutting a deep gash to the west. (Australian-sounding, but almost Himalayan-looking: an outstanding evening stroll for those stopping off at Seathwaite.) Most striking is the rich blend of greens of every shade that make the Duddon valley so distinctive. Wordsworth quite rightly acclaimed this as one of the most beautiful valleys in England.

The path deteriorates as centuries of rainfall have washed away the surface on the two-mile descent to Seathwaite. Many old mines are passed as the path runs to the left of a gully. The track becomes tarred at the valley floor. A public footpath on the left doubles back through two fields to Turner Hall Farm (campsite, and a nice one).

The path circumvents the farm to the right to reach another lane. Go straight ahead at the gate and turn left on reaching the narrow road to Ulpha. There are some waterfalls and a riverside path beside the road on the right. Continue to a sharp right hand bend just short of Seathwaite. The village has a good pub (the Newfield Inn).

The route leaves the road through the gate to the left, where a boulder track climbs to the Dunnerdale Fells. There is a wall to the right while the jagged slopes of Caw rise to the left. Beyond Caw, take the right fork, a track that contours into a small bandit-infested col at which point the estuary comes into sight. (Well, the col feels bandit-infested.) At GR 218933 we turn right again on a grass cart track and climb 20m (50ft) to the top of a hill looking across a minor road to Stickle Pike.

Cross the lane at its highest point (by a small parking area) to the path on the other side. The track splits into two: take the left one. A gradual rise curling left suddenly reveals Stickle Tarn, a concealed reed-strangled pool. While there is an indistinct line to the left of the tarn, a better path is found 10m (30ft) above this line.

Before taking either, the short detour to the top of Stickle Pike is a must. Its isolated position means wide views from the plump well-packed cairn. The path from Seathwaite can be traced as it weaves among the debris of the disused quarries. Ahead, bold green paths

Descending the little track beneath Caw, with Stickle Pike ahead

lead to the coastline where, we hope, sunlight shimmers on the roofs of houses.

From the top of Stickle Pike return to the higher of the two paths and turn right, keeping parallel to and about 15m (50ft) above Stickle Tarn. Then head south alongside Red Moss Beck. Yes, the ground really is red and mossy here. At least with green bits you know the light greens are nice and the dark greens are not so nice. Keep to the right of the marshy bowl at the base of the rising ground. The path becomes more pronounced as it carves a course downward through the bracken. Go through a gate and follow the green lane between two dilapidated walls down to the small copse (look out for robbers!) A path through the trees leads to Green Bank and a short stroll along the road on the left brings you to Broughton Mills.

5: Broughton Mills to Foxfield: 4 miles/6km

With no hills left to climb over, the run-out to the estuary is field paths, with the occasional small wood or waterfall. The highlight of the section is the delightful small town of Broughton in Furness.

The Blacksmith's Arms with its log fires and low beamed ceilings dates back to the 17th-century and claims to be the oldest in the Lakes. It's just up the lane to Broughton in Furness for those who are thirsty. Otherwise follow the signposted path on the near side of the River Lickle. It follows the river at first then maintains its direction across fields where the river makes one of its lazy loops. Path and river are soon reacquainted for a short way by some pleasant waterfalls, then the path goes its own way to the lane at Croglinhurst.

Turn left along the lane then go to left of Hartley Ground farm by a narrow, stony and waterlogged path. As the path comes out into open pastures follow a line of holly and hawthorn trees rising towards Hagg farm. Then keep on the right of the woods, maintaining a straight line through three more fields. The gaps in the walls get progressively narrower and the last one must surely be sponsored by Weight Watchers.

Cross the road and enter the next field, raking across to the right almost parallel with the road. A cinder track leading towards Broughton Tower is followed left for 15yds before crossing an iron stile on the right. Turn left between the trees and the waterless tarn and pass along to the right of the school grounds. In the left corner of the field is a wooden fence and stile; the path beyond leads into the market square of Broughton in Furness.

Broughton is a captivating little town with a Georgian market square. The stocks, the fish slabs and a memorial to the Jubilee of King George III stand in the centre beneath chestnut trees. The town boasts antique, craft and walking shops, but more importantly a wealth of cafes, B&Bs, and fine inns.

Head left, following the main Lancaster road as far as the primary school. Opposite it is a narrow lane, part of the Cumbria Way. As the lane begins to rise we are treated to a splendid view of the charming little town. Grey and white cottages with smoky chimneys are sunken into rolling green pastures. Out on a limb is the chubby little Saxon church looking out to sea.

As the lane bends left we are left facing a whitewashed cottage. Here the signposted path turns off left under some trees, to a golf course belonging to a large hotel. Go to right of the hotel, then swing left on a field path to another narrow lane near Coal Gate. Head south on the lane beneath Foxfield Bank into Foxfield village.

There's not much to Foxfield: a railway station, pub and a signal box – and if the tide's out, the sea could be as much as ten miles away down the Duddon estuary. Rather than walk the ten miles of shifting quicksand, it seems simpler to stop in the pub and wait for the sea to come to you; then the train to take you out.

SUNSHINE HIGH-LINES: if the sun should, by some chance, be shining, walkers may want to set their sights higher. After Sandwick, an ascent can be made of Place Fell, with a descent by way of Boredale Hause to Hartsop. That high-level route is actually almost as nice as the lakeside path... On the second day, the ascent over St Sunday Crag and Cofa Pike to Fairfield is splendid, with a ridge-walk over Hart Crag and High Pike to Ambleside. If the sun still continued to shine, I would climb onto the Coniston range by way of Levers Water to Levers Hause before crossing Dow Crag. For those still vigorous after fifty miles, there's Black Combe waiting at the end of the walk.

ACCOMMODATION, SHOPS, PUBS: Penrith, Lowther Park (shop), Askham (pubs, shop), Howtown (inn), Patterdale, Brotherswater (inn, bunkhouse, camp-site), Ambleside, Loughrigg (campsite), Skelwith Bridge (inns), Elterwater, Colwith Force (High Park B&B), Coniston, Seathwaite (Newfield Inn, camp site), Broughton Mills (Inn), Broughton-in-Furness.

TRAVEL: Penrith is on the London Euston to Glasgow main railway line while Foxfield is on the Carlisle-Barrow-Carnforth railway line.

On Going Twice As Far

Anyone planning the walk of the Lakes Threethousands is either absurdly over ambitious or else already accustomed to normal day-walks on British mountains. While I have a lot of sympathy for absurd overambition, the notes below assume you already have basic hill skills (such as an understanding of contour lines and the compass) and know what to wear and carry for a walk of ordinary, sensible length.

Sometimes such walkers manage not to enjoy – or not to complete – the walk that's twice that sensible distance. Leaving aside bad weather, bad route-finding, too much luggage, knee injury, ankle injury, exhaustion and equipment failure, three mistakes that could have been avoided were: not enough eating, not enough drinking, and too much speed.

START SLOWLY: Don't try to walk faster than usual. Walk just slightly slower than usual. You can speed up later on, if you feel like it (you won't). But if you're walking too fast at first, you'll start suffering before you're even half way. The main reason for the schedules we have included is to warn you when you're going too fast.

On the other hand -

STOP STOPPING. Which is easier: to walk at two miles and hour, or to jog at four miles an hour and then stand still? The logic is obvious: stopping for a rest is a waste of energy.

Stopping for the sandwiches is one of the small pleasures of a mountain day. But when you're going for the big one, small pleasures are done without. Nibble as you go along – it's perfectly possible to get through a bar of chocolate and two cheese sandwiches on the way up Helvellyn.

The average walker spends ten minutes in the hour fiddling about in the ruck-sack. Wear a bumbag at the front (which turns it into a tumbag). Put in it the hat, gloves, some Tracker bars, the map and perhaps a very tiny camera. (But not the compass: compasses fall out of bumbags.)

EAT LOTS: If you're doing two walks at once, do you need two lunches? No. You need at least three lunches. As a rough guide, the Lakes Threethousands require 4000 Calories (nearly 20,000 kJ) and 4000 Calories weigh a kilogram not counting fruit. Don't say "I'll save that till later." Say "I'll see if I can get that down now, and then another one." Keep eating at least to Thirlspot and avoid that flake-out of the final five miles.

DRINK LOTS: Dehydration doesn't feel like thirst, it feels like tiredness. You may be feeling tired anyway – but perhaps it isn't exhaustion at all. On a really sunny day you could need as much as three litres to keep the body operating properly.

No Business Like Snow Business

When you undertake a long-distance challenge in the depths of Winter, you wind up both the satisfaction and the suffering by several notches.

You do need to be Winter competent before undertaking Winter challenges. The Winter of 1997, when we ran the Threethousands, was untypical. Usually Winter means snow, and snow means ice axes. The skill of stopping a slide with the ice-axe is a fairly simple one – much easier than riding a bicycle – but does need to be mastered by all Winter walkers. On hard refrozen snow or ice, crampons are used. I've even found crampons necessary on frozen gravel scree in Lord's Rake.

The National Park Rangers' telephone weather forecast includes very valuable information on felltop conditions and any avalanche risk. Cornices form at the top of steep lee slopes, such as the east face of Helvellyn. These pose a particular risk in white-out, or when long days have stretched on into the Winter night.

Only fairly eccentric people will want to undertake the Threethousands or the Old County Tops in Winter – although the Bob Graham Round has been completed at least twice under snow and ice. The great Horseshoe walks are outstanding under snow: the Eskdale and Langdale ones are comparatively short but have lots of mountaineering interest.

A low-level expedition like the Penrith crossing can be particularly good in the off-season, with ice on the lakes, frost on the branches and a log fire in the bar. Take an ice-axe anyway: sunshine and snow on the tops make it impossible to stick to a planned valley route.

It's one of my unfulfilled ambitions to attempt the Roman Road crossing from Penrith to Windermere on cross-country (Nordic) skis.

Running Business

People come into fellrunning from two directions. Some of us are fellwalkers who speeded up; others are road-runners who've had enough of roads. (Fellrunning's gentler than road-running; the hills mean you don't have to go flat out all the time. Fellrunning is also easier on the knees.)

The ex-roadrunners look in astonishment at all the luggage carried by the ex-fellwalkers. The ex-fellwalkers look in horror at all the luggage not carried by the ex-roadrunners.

On a fell race, there are other runners around (at least until the point where you get lost, last, or injured), and maybe people with radios as well. Under these conditions it is perhaps not excessively unsafe to run around in what is, basically, your underwear. Even so, fell racers are required to carry full waterproof body cover and a few ounces of emergency food, as well as map and compass and whistle.

For the run of the 3000s, considerably more food than this will be needed: the 4000 Cal (1kg) suggested for walkers will also feed runners.

A runner who's only keeping warm by keeping running is taking a risk. If injury, exhaustion or getting lost leads to a drop in speed, death by exposure is uncomfortably close. A half-naked, stationary runner in really foul weather will not necessarily survive long enough to get rescued.

That's the ex-fellwalker's perspective, and very sensible it is too. However, the ex-roadrunner points out, quite rightly, that the main reason we can run not walk is (not our super-tuned fitness and sticky-out muscles) but small rucksacks and light little shoes. The hills are smaller for runners, and if necessary you really could reach the road in ninety minutes.

I'm an ex-fellwalker. I say: suppose you do decide to drop out at Dunmail. How are you going to feel catching the Keswick bus in pink-and-yellow shorts and a snot-covered tee shirt that says FELL-RUNNERS DO IT ON TOP?

The Bob Graham Round

While the Threethousands may be Lakeland's supreme challenge for walkers, its supreme challenge for runners is the Bob Graham Round. Bob Graham held the record for most-peaks-in-24hrs from 1936 to 1961. His trip over 42 tops is still the longest hill run that the ordinary fellrunner can reasonably hope to complete, given good weather, good luck, and reasonable dedication to training.

The run starts and finishes at the Moot Hall, Keswick at any hour of the day or night, and may be taken in either direction. The following summits are to be visited: THE BOB GRAHAM 42: KESWICK (MOOT HALL): Skiddaw, Great Calva, Blencathra: THRELKELD: Clough Head, Great Dodd, Watson's Dodd, Stybarrow Dodd, Raise, Whiteside, Low Man, Helvellyn, Nethermost Pike, Dollywaggon Pike, Fairfield, Seat Sandal: DUNMAIL RAISE: Steel End, Calf Crag, Sergeant Man, High Raise, Thunacar Knott, Harrison Stickle, Pike of Stickle, Rossett Pike, Bowfell, Esk Pike, Great End, Ill Crag, Broad Crag, Scafell Pike, Scafell: WASDALE: Yewbarrow, Red Pike, Steeple, Pillar, Kirk Fell, Great Gable, Green Gable, Brandreth, Grey Knotts: HONISTER: Dale Head, Hindscarth, Robinson: KESWICK. *See map on page 14.*

A runner belonging to one of the main North of England fellrunning clubs (Ambleside, Dark Peak) will be able to avail himself or herself of the club's Bob Graham Machine: a well-oiled assembly of experienced runners who know the route, know the correct pace, carry the luggage and urge you onward with frightful curses when you attempt to flake out on Great Gable.

If you don't have such a machine at your disposal, do not despair. More rewarding, to my mind, is to take control of your own destiny. Work out the schedule that suits you, and do your own exploring. The spring days I spent, running 20-mile or 30-mile chunks of Lakeland, are still among the best I've known. There was the February day when we crossed Scafell Pike with snow over the boulders, and snow also over the nasty screes of Lord's Rake. "Not trainers," we told them in the gully: "not trainers, these are fell-running shoes." This was one of the few occasions when I've combined rubber studs underfoot with ice axe in hand. "What the hell," we told each other, and dropped into Wasdale, and so night fell on us while we were still on Steeple. We picked our way along Moses Trod above a deep Ennerdale full of darkness, and came down from Honister by the feel of the tarmac underfoot. Which meant, of course, coming back for Kirk Fell – and that was another lovely run, in cool sun and clear air, and down to Buttermere for a quick head-in-the-Lake.

Then, finally, there was Bob Graham day itself. For many, Bob Graham Day is a very, very horrible one. I was lucky with weather (just slightly too hot), with injuries (leg ligaments gave no trouble at all for the entire first half of the run), and with clever companions who stopped me rushing away along the Helvellyn ridge. And Bob Graham Day was one of the best days ever.

The hints that follow are intended to save some time and trouble, while not depriving the independent adventurer of the pleasure of getting it all worked out.

SUPPORT: While the Bob Graham is just achievable, the Bob Graham with ten pound rucksack just isn't. Unless you're supremely talented and fit, you'll need a friendly car at the road crossings, and a companion carrying water and Tracker bars on the hill.

DIRECTION OF TRAVEL: 1000ft of up takes the same time on boulders as on gentle grass. 1000ft of grass is, on the other hand, much quicker to go down than the boulders are. Therefore the better direction has steep scree and boulders uphill mostly. So I favour clockwise.

START TIME: Uphill is no slower in the dark, and neither is road. Off Skiddaw is uniform heather where it doesn't matter where you put your foot. So I favour 2am.

SCHEDULE: The most important thing is not to start off too fast. The relative times of the five sections should be

Keswick – Threlkeld (with Skiddaw)	4hr 50
Threlkeld – Dunmail (with Helvellyn)	4hr 20
Dunmail Raise to Wasdale (with Scafells)	6hr 05
Wasdale to Honister (with Gt Gable)	5hr 05
Honister to Keswick (Derwent Fells, road)	3hr 10
rests: less, if possible, than	1hr 10
TOTAL	23hr 40

ROUTE CLUES

* Dollywaggon-Fairfield: from the outflow of Grisedale Tarn an eroded path runs straight upslope onto Fairfield. This is the one path in Lakeland at which we look in horror and say: that erosion is totally down to runners on the Round. (Straight up-and-down paths on steep places are the quick way, once the water gets in, to tear open the slope.) I don't like this on moral grounds. But also, I think the way above the head of the tarn to Grisedale Hause is quicker.

* Seat Sandal-Honister: in this direction, the straight way down the ridge is

quicker than the path by Raise Beck. However, it's crucial to come off the end at the right place to avoid steep ground.
* High Raise: some do Sergeant Man before High Raise.
* Pike of Stickle to Rossett Pike: the direct route across the beck is quicker than round by Stake Pass.
* Rossett Pike-Bowfell: a direct route slants up by Hanging Knotts. Use your one clear recce day here – from the summit of Rossett the line up the broken face is obvious.
* Scafell – Scafell Pike: the rock climb of Broad Stand saves eight minutes over Lord's Rake and West Wall Traverse. The climb is intimidating, but not actually difficult if you've practised it beforehand with a rope.
* Pillar to Kirk Fell: take the rocky spur of Kirk Fell direct from Black Sail Pass.
* Robinson to Keswick: the ridge of High Snab Bank is the quick way off. Given daylight, paths from Skelghyll are an alternative to road.

FORETHOUGHT: Mood-swings during the run can make you give up when actually going quite well, or irrationally hope to claw back two lost hours on the ascent of Great Gable. So decide whether a 25-hour round is worth achieving, or if you prefer to pull out while you still have legs under you in hope of a re-run later in the year. Calculate in advance how far behind schedule you can fall and still reasonably retain hope.

FAILURE: Second attempts in August rarely succeed. You're still tired from last time, the bracken and heather are higher, and it's liable to be far too hot.

Nightwalking

When you climb high mountains in the Alps, you always start in the dark. You rise at two, or at one, and peer out of the windows. You can't see any stars, which means the weather's not good enough and you can get right back into that warm sleeping bag, but then someone points out that the reason there are no stars is that the window has shutters on the outside... So you try to eat something, and two-day-old French bread at two in the morning could well be the worst breakfast ever. You pull on your boots (and if you think you've stiffened up in the night, then just feel what your boots have done) and stumble down the moraine by torchlight.

And then you get onto the glacier. In the night the glacier's frozen crisp as cornflakes, and the moon lights it up like a motorway so you don't need the torch. You speed up, and warm up, and at the head of the glacier your mountain makes a sharp shape against the stars. The bottom edge of the sky goes all indigo, then rosy pink, and the first sun touches the high rocks. And soon you'll be having another breakfast on some warm ledge up there, and wondering what's happened to the bread to make it taste so much better than it did four hours ago.

One of the distinctions of the Lakes Threethousands is the way it offers you, in the security and comfort of your own home country, the joys of the Alpine Start. You miss out on the crispness of the early glacier, but the rest of it is there: the silence of the night mountain, the view reduced to outlines and pools of black, the gradual arrival of the light and then the sudden sun. You also get, of course, the unappetising torchlit breakfast: it's an essential part of the package.

Skiddaw is a very suitable mountain to do in the dark. After the first, wooded, section, you reach the Latrigg car park, and now the path is broad and clear. On a clear moonlit night it may seem almost like daytime except they forgot to press the colour control. Even a clear starlit night, or a clouded moonlit one, will let you switch off the torch and adjust your eyesight to the dark.

A torch will, however, still be needed. Distances shift in the dark: that mountain on the horizon is actually a knoll 50yds away. The wide and obvious way is not so obvious in the moonlight. It's not that the fairies have taken the path away or bent it; path detection depends on colour vision. So a torch will still be needed for map-and-compass work. The other requirement is an extra layer of clothing. It's cold up there, and also you'll be moving slower than you usually do.

Don't plan to arrive at Skiddaw summit any earlier than dawn. Downhill in the dark is not nice at all. But uphill in the dark: that is nice. And sunrise on Skiddaw is just as good as sunset on Helvellyn's going to be.

Usefulness Of The Moon

The full moon is also the moon that rises at sunset and sets at sunrise. So it's doubly useful. The new moon is not only invisible, it's only up during the daytime, so doubly useless. The waxing moon is in the sky at sunset, and sets at some point during the night. During the week before full moon, it will be in the sky at least until midnight, and usefully bright. The waning moon is in the sky for the later part of the night, until dawn.

For the Threethousands, the ideal will be the night of full moon, or up to a week after: this will give useful light for Skiddaw. For the Old County Tops, ideal moon is up to a week before the full: this will light you back to Grasmere if you go too slowly and night falls. However, you'll always need a torch under the trees on Red Bank.

The Threethousands With The Ramblers' Association

Most of the people who achieve the four Threethousands do so thanks to the Ramblers' Association. The first of their organised walks was in 1965, with Bill Stanton as Race Secretary. 83 tough walkers, most of them in boots and breeches, set out from Keswick bus station.

The weather was friendly, and about half of the 83 finished the course. First home was Stan Bradshaw in 11 hrs 11 minutes, a clear hour ahead of the field. It is notable that his age at the time – 51 years – was more than the combined ages of the next two finishers! First lady was 18-year-old Ruth Mingins in 18 hrs 20 min. The prizes were presented by Mrs MY Wakefield – Lakeland Area President of the RA, and the widow of Dr AW Wakefield whose Threethousands exploit is described in the history chapter.

The event has been held every year since, except 1997 when there were administrative difficulties (the organisers would always like to hear from anyone keen to crouch in a tent at Sty Head!) Today the race entries are limited to 250. About half might call themselves runners; far fewer regard the event as a competitive race. Of those who do, the fastest so far has been Billy Bland, who recorded 7 hr 35 min in 1979. He and Joss Naylor both passed Steel End too early for any checkpoint food.

The walk takes place on the third Saturday in June, and is open to members of the Ramblers' Association and of affiliated clubs (which include the Long Distance Walkers' Association). There is a minimum age of 16 years; walkers aged 18 or under must be accompanied. There is no maximum age, and walkers in their seventies attract no particular comment. The start is at 2am from Keswick Rugby Club.

There are check-points at
Skiddaw summit: Keswick Moot Hall
Seathwaite Farm: FOOD: TIME POINT 9:00am
Sty Head Pass: Scafell summit: Scafell Pike summit:
Esk Hause: TIME POINT 2:30pm
High Raise
Steel End: FOOD: TIME POINT 6:00pm
Helvellyn Summit: Stanah bus shelter
Keswick: FOOD: TIME POINT 12:00 midnight.

Any route may be taken between checkpoints except that walkers may use Lord's Rake in ascent only. Entrants failing to make the time points must retire.

The main advantages of an organised event are companionship, the useful food, the extra safety cover, and the fact that it's on a particular date so that you have to do it and not dither. The particular day may well be a nasty one – but the comradeship and encouragement probably outweigh this. So you get round anyway, and have a much more interesting story to tell, if worse photos.

The main disadvantage is that time cut-off at Seathwaite. Walkers who are not runners should be very disciplined, resist all temptation to speed down

Above the clouds on Cofa Pike

Borrowdale, and aim to get through the checkpoint as near to the last minute as possible.

For an entry form, send stamped addressed envelope to Barbara Hall, Lea Croft, Hunsonby, Penrith CA10 1PN

Schedule for the Lakes 3000s

	miles	km	hrs:min	ETA	
Keswick				0200	
Skiddaw	5	8	2:30	0430	1
Portinscale	9½	15	1:30	0600	2
Hollows Farm	14½	23	1:00	0700	3
Seathwaite	18	29	1:30	0830	3
Scafell	23	37	3:00	1130	4
Scafell Pike	24	38.5	1:00	1230	
High Raise	29	46.5	2:00	1430	5
Wythburn Church	33½	53.5	1:15	1545	
Helvellyn	35½	57	2:00	1745	
Legburnthwaite	39	62.5	1:15	1900	
Keswick	45	72	2:00	2100	6
Total climb:	11,000 ft	3300m			

NOTES:
1: Restraint! Too fast here spoils chances
2: Downhill skills vary. Too fast or too slow here won't affect outcome.
3: Restraint! Do not exceed schedule's speed limit in Borrowdale.
4: Not exhausted at Scafell means chances good, irrespective of time
5: 1hr before sunset here is latest to ensure daylight for Wythburn
6: Measurement off map, as used elsewhere in this book, gives distance of 42 miles. For once, we have adopted the common practice of adding 5% 'for wiggles' to get the traditional 45-mile distance.

Schedule for the Old County Tops

These timings are for a strong walker aiming to do it in daylight.

	miles	km	hrs:min	ETA
Grasmere				0600
Helvellyn	5½	9	2:30	0830
Wythburn Church	7½	13	0:40	0910
High Raise	12	19	2:00	1110
Scafell Pikes	16	26	1:50	1300
Cockley Beck	21	33	1:40	1440
Coniston Old Man	25½	41	2:40	1720
Little Langdale	31	50	2:20	2000
Grasmere	35	56	1:30	2130
Total time			15½ hrs	
Total climb:	10,000ft	3600m		

What Next?

Some, having accomplished the Lakes Threethousands or the Old County Tops, will collapse back into ordinary fell walking. If we need to boast we now have something to boast about, and there's more to enjoy than mere distance and speed. There is pleasure to be gained from lunch sitting down, and paddling in tarns, and long evenings with beer in, and looking at wild flowers, and sketching in watercolours, and not having very big blisters.

However, there's also a lot of fun in fast and far, and leave the watercolours till later in life. For those who want more enormous walks, here's a quick round up of the best in Britain.

The Lyke Wake Walk
40 miles, 4000ft
This east-west crossing of the North York Moors has had some – but not all – of its mud trudge eliminated by path repairs. This has made it slightly less challenging, but a lot more pleasurable. It's a varied mix of hill and moorland, across country that's unfamiliar to many. Those who achieve the walk within 24 hrs are entitled to join the Lyke Wake Club. The popularity of the walk has led to severe erosion on the peat moorland, and walkers are asked not to attempt it in particularly soggy weather or in large groups. Guidebook: *Lyke Wake Walk and the Lyke Wake Way*: from Lyke Wake Club, PO Box 24, Northallerton DL6 3HZ

The Yorkshire Three Peaks
24 miles, 5000ft
This crosses the three most impressive hills of Yorkshire – OK that still doesn't make them all that impressive, but it's interesting limestone landscape. And the walk, for a long one, is unusually short, which may account in part for its popularity. The other part is successful publicity by the Pen-y-ghent Cafe, Horton, which is the traditional start and endpoint and which issues certificates and badges for completions under 12 hours. The three relevant peaks are Pen-y-ghent, Whernside, and Ingleborough. (Runners' record? You really don't want to know. All right then: 2 hr 46 min.)
Guidebook: *Peaks of the Yorkshire Dales* (John Gillham and Phil Iddon, Grey Stone Books)

The Welsh Threethousands
28 miles, 15,000ft
This is the Lakes 3000s with the valley bits left out: the route crosses low ground at just two points, and is otherwise high mountain ground of the most rugged and interesting sort. It culminates in the serious ridge-scramble of Crib Goch. The Welsh Threes is the only long walk south of Scotland that I consider to be definitely better than the Lakes Threes or even the Old County Tops. Runners' record: 4 hr 21.
Guidebook: *The Welsh Three Thousand Foot Challenges* (Roy Clayton and Ronald Turnbull: Grey Stone Books 1997)

Tranter's Walk

38 miles, 21,000ft

Perhaps the ultimate long walk (anything longer being a long run), this starts on Ben Nevis, crosses the famous Arete to Carn Mor Dearg and the Grey Corries; then returns over the Mamores range to Glen Nevis. The recent revision has reduced its nineteen Munros to eighteen, but done nothing to reduce the appeal of its three scrambling sections, its swooping high ridges, its quartzite, granite and grass. The route crosses no road, and is exposed to snow on any day of the year. The ascent is equivalent to Scafell Pike from Seatoller seven times.

No guidebook, and anyone contemplating this walk should be experienced enough not to need one. For awkward route-finding on Aonach Beag: *Britain's Highest Peaks* (Jeremy Ashcroft, David & Charles)

The Four now Five Fourthousanders (Cairngorms)

21 miles, 8000ft

This may seem a great deal shorter than the Lakes Threethousands. However, it is close to the 4000ft (1300m) contour for the greater part of the distance, and penetrates into the heart of the most inhospitable country in Britain. While the high plateau offers fast and easy walking, the same cannot be said for the 2000 feet down and up again at the crossing of the Lairig Ghru. The record for runners is set at 4hr 34 for men, 6 hr 45 for women; the men's record dates from 1979, and the very vigorous should note that it is the least unbreakable of those listed here. The recent revision of Munro's Tables has increased the Four Fourthousanders to five.

Again, no guidebook.

The Cuillin Ridge

14 miles, 13,000 ft

with the runners' record at 3 hrs 22 mins; these figures don't suggest a big walk. And what we have here is indeed not a big walk: it's a very big mountaineering expedition on the Isle of Skye, with rock climbing up to the grade of V Diff and very little that's less than a scramble. Though footpath erosion will never be a problem on this all-rock route, its popularity means that on fine weekends you can expect to queue – possibly for several hours – at the first serious climb at the Thearlaich-Dubh gap.

Guidebook:: *Scrambles on Skye* (J Wilson Parker, Cicerone)

Data Section

Tourist Information:

All Cumbria: Windermere Tel: 015394 44444

Local and seasonal: Ambleside 015394 32582 and 40404; Grasmere 015394 35245; Pooley Bridge 017684 86530; Keswick 017687 72645

Lake District National Park Authority, Brockhole, Windermere Tel: 015394 46601

Data Section – Continued

Weather Forecasts:

1-day, with felltop conditions 01768 775757
5-day 0891 500319

Shelter and Food:

Youth Hostels: the larger hostels, in the towns and villages, are full during the Summer. The remote, off-road ones (Skiddaw, Black Sail, Coniston Coppermines, etc) are closed on some days of the week. Either way, contact individual hostels – we've marked their positions on the route maps. General YHA info from 01727 845215
Camping: wild camping above the enclosed ground is accepted provided it is done sensitively. Camp sites in the villages tend to be full (also rather expensive). Farm sites with lower prices and lower facilities usually have space. Of these, we have found Hollows Farm, Borrowdale and Turner Hall Farm, Dunnerdale to be particularly good.
Camping Barns: information and bookings from Keswick Tourist Information
Good Pubs: Careful counting might discover a hundred good pubs in the Lake District. Our own choice is always the closest one we haven't been to before. We haven't been disappointed yet. Among our favourites are: the Newfield Inn, Seathwaite, Duddon Valley; the Blacksmiths Arms, Broughton Mills; the Queens Head, Askham; the Howton Hotel, Ullswater; the Fish, Buttermere; the Sun, Coniston and the Royal Dockray, Ullswater

Events:

* Ramblers Association *Lakes Threethousands*: Contact Barbara Hall, Lea Croft, Hunsonby, Penrith, CA10 1PN
* *Great Lakeland Challenge*: 100 miles of hills over 3 days of early May bank holiday. Contact Bowscar Centre, Plumpton, Penrith, CA11 9NP
* *Old County Tops Race*: for pairs of experienced fellrunners. Contact A Daniels, Schoolhouse, Ferney Lee Road, Todmorden, OL14 5NR

Organisations:

* Long Distance Walkers' Association: Contact Janet Chapman, 63 Yockley Close, The Maultway, Camberley, Surrey GU15 1QQ
* Ramblers' Association: 1-5 Wandsworth Rd, London SW8 2XX
* Fell Runners' Association: Pete Bland, 34a Kirkland, Kendal, Cumbria LA9 5AD
* British Trust for Conservation Volunteers: 36 St Mary's St, Wallingford, Oxon OX10 0EU
* Friends of the Lake District (charity working to protect and preserve the Lake District) Freepost LA1186 Kendal LA9 8BR

Transport:

Rail: 0345 48 49 50
Buses: Stagecoach Cumbria 01946 63222 or Cumbria travelline 01228 606000

Mountain Rescue: 999 and ask for Mountain Rescue Service